The *Professional Education* of *Teachers*

A PERCEPTUAL VIEW OF TEACHER PREPARATION

Arthur W. Combs

UNIVERSITY OF FLORIDA

ALLYN AND BACON, INC.   BOSTON

© Copyright 1965 by Allyn and Bacon, Inc.
470 Atlantic Avenue, Boston, Massachusetts

 All rights reserved. No portion of this book may be reproduced in any form, or by any means, without permission in writing from the publisher.

Library of Congress Catalog Card Number: 65-15937
Printed in the United States of America

Eighth Printing . . . March, 1970

Preface

AFTER YEARS OF TAKING IT FOR GRANTED, we have suddenly discovered that education is not merely useful but absolutely necessary for our way of life. To keep the world we live in running requires the production of intelligent people in ever-increasing numbers. Education has become essential to survival! As a consequence, people everywhere are taking a good hard look at our public schools to find out if they truly meet our needs.

Some of the improvements we seek in education can be brought about by spending more money, by building better schools, by introducing new courses of study, new standards, or new equipment. But the really important changes will only come about as teachers change. Institutions are made up of people, and it is the behavior of teachers in classrooms that will finally determine whether or not our schools meet or fail to meet the challenge of our times. It is at the source of supply—in our teacher-preparation programs—that review and innovation are most critically called for if we are to bring about the improvements we need in education.

The crucial role of these programs has not been overlooked. The full glare of public scrutiny has been turned upon them, resulting in a flood of comment and criticism in speeches, pamphlets, books, and articles from persons in every walk of life. Many of these have done little more than "view with alarm." Others have voiced the deep and honest concern of citizens for better teaching of our youth. Some have had political axes to grind or vested interests to stump for. A few, like the Conant Report,[1] the ASCD Commission Report,[2] or the

[1] Conant, J. B. *The Education of American Teachers* (New York: McGraw-Hill, 1963).

[2] Denemark, G. W., ed. *Criteria for Curriculum Decisions in Teacher Education* (Washington, D. C.: Association for Supervision and Curriculum Development, N.E.A., 1964).

continuing work of NCTEPS,[3] have been careful, thoughtful studies carried out by qualified and dedicated people. The product of all this effort and discussion, however, has so far been bitterly disappointing. For the most part it has resulted in little more than a reshuffling of the same old courses, a heavier load of content for teacher-education students, and some changes in procedures for certification and licensing of teachers. This is not enough.

Teacher education needs much more than a tinkering job. What is called for is a re-examination of the problem in the light of our changing social needs and purposes on the one hand, and our new understandings about human behavior and learning on the other. A modern philosophical-psychological base is needed on which to base our thinking and experimentation. Fortunately, it seems to be at hand.

These are exciting times in the social sciences. Within the past twenty years a whole series of new concepts about man and his behavior has appeared upon the scene. This social science break-through has resulted from the emergence in American psychology of a great new humanistic force, a new psychology deeply concerned with people, values, perceptions, and man's eternal search for being and becoming. The impact of these new ideas is powerful indeed. They promise new solutions to age-old human problems. Already they have profoundly influenced the work of several other professions. Little by little as they find their way into education, they promise similar revolutions for teaching and learning. Where these ideas will eventually lead us, no one can say, but this much is certain: No profession charged with responsibilities for human welfare will ever be the same, for, whenever our ideas about the nature of man change, great changes are called for in the ways we live and work with people. This is especially so for teaching, the most human profession of all.

It has been my good fortune for nearly twenty-five years to be deeply involved in this new psychology and with teacher education as well. From this vantage point I have been more and more impressed with the widespread implications this new way of looking at human behavior has for every aspect of teacher preparation. For three years as editor of the 1962 ASCD Yearbook, *Perceiving, Behaving, Becoming*,[4] I explored the meaning of a few of these ideas for teaching with

---

[3] *New Horizons*, Report of the National Commission on Teacher Education and Professional Standards (Washington, D. C.: N.E.A., 1964).

[4] (Washington, D. C.: Association for Supervision and Curriculum Development, 1962).

a national committee of professional educators. The results of those deliberations and the reception they have had from the profession have convinced me that this new psychology has far-reaching implications for teacher education. It ought to be translated into educational practice with the least possible delay.

That is the reason for this book. I have not attempted to design a comprehensive teacher-education program. That is a local problem to be worked out by particular faculties charged with teacher-education responsibilities. Instead, I have tried in this book to look at the professional aspects of undergraduate, pre-service teacher education through a new set of glasses provided by modern thinking in perceptual-existential psychology. Seen in this way, some traditional practices are corroborated; that is comfortable. Some long-held traditions are also brought into question; that is distressing. Most important of all, new things are suggested that promise much for the future, and that is exciting!

A book is always a product of the author's interaction with the ideas and personalities of other people, and this one is no exception. It would be quite impossible for me to name all those people who, knowingly or not, have contributed to the ideas presented here. Nevertheless, I am deeply grateful to them. To the graduate students who have worked with me over the last ten years I owe a great deal for the testing and molding of concepts provided by their "loyal opposition" and for the hard work and intelligence they have so enthusiastically devoted to our research. I am especially indebted to four of my friends and colleagues who carefully read and commented on the manuscript during its production:

Dr. Joyce Cooper, Professor of Education, my colleague in the College of Education, University of Florida;

Dr. Earl Kelley, Professor of Education, Wayne State University, my very good friend and source of much inspiration;

Dr. Joseph B. White, Dean of the College of Education, University of Florida, who originally suggested the preparation of this manuscript; and

Richard Usher, officially my graduate assistant but also valued and respected friend, critic, and collaborator in this and other research and writing projects.

ARTHUR W. COMBS

Contents

1 WHAT IS A GOOD TEACHER?   1
  The teacher as knower
  The "competencies" approach to teaching
  The personal character of good teaching
  The "self as instrument" concept

2 A PERCEPTUAL VIEW OF EFFECTIVE TEACHING   10
  Third force psychology
  The helping relationship
  The perceptual view of effective teaching

3 CREATING EFFECTIVE TEACHERS   25
  Creating effective practitioners
  The perceptual view of effective learning
  The need for commitment
  The conditions for effective learning

4 THE GOOD TEACHER IS WELL INFORMED   39
  The selection of content
  The teaching of content

5 THE TEACHER'S BELIEFS ABOUT PEOPLE   54
  The effective teacher's concepts about people
  Helping students formulate adequate concepts
    about people

6 THE TEACHER'S SELF   68
  The self of the effective teacher
  Producing teachers with adequate personalities

7   THE TEACHER'S PURPOSES   82

    The purposes of effective teachers
    The inadequacy of formal courses for discovering
        purpose
    The problems approach to discovering purposes
    The use of discussion groups for exploration of
        purposes

8   THE PERSONAL DISCOVERY OF WAYS TO TEACH   98

    A facilitating, encouraging atmosphere
    Personal involvement with students and teaching
    Rich opportunities to explore and discover appropriate
        teaching techniques

9   ORGANIZING THE PROFESSIONAL ASPECTS OF A
    TEACHER-PREPARATION PROGRAM   112

    The inadequacy of organization around content
    The need for flexibility
    A proposal for organization
    Administrative problems of organization
    Student evaluation

1

What Is a
Good Teacher?

WHATEVER WE DO IN TEACHER EDUCATION must depend on our having some idea of the nature of good teaching. To plan effective programs we need the very best definitions of good teaching we can get. That seems clear enough. How to arrive at such definitions, however, has proven a most difficult problem. Despite millions of dollars and millions of man hours poured into research on the problem over the past fifty years, the results have continued to be frustrating and disappointing—until recently.

It now appears that our failure to find useful definitions may be due to the fact that we have been looking for answers in the wrong places. For several generations teacher-education programs have operated with a concept of good teaching derived from the mechanistic view of behavior characteristic of American psychology during the past fifty years. Now a new psychology has appeared on the scene which shifts our understanding of people from a mechanistic to a humanistic view. Applied to the problem of defining good teaching, this new frame of reference seems to provide us with better answers to our old problem. To put the matter in perspective, however, let us begin with a look at where we have been.

THE TEACHER AS KNOWER

The earliest conception of the good teacher was that of the scholar. It was assumed that a person who knew could teach others. Of course it is true that a teacher has to know something, but even without research it is apparent to anyone who looks that knowing is simply not enough. Most of us can recall out of our own experience the teacher

1

who "knew his subject but couldn't put it across." In some places there can even be found good teachers whose depth of information in a particular field is woefully lacking. This is often a shocking discovery to some critics of education who still equate teaching with scholarship. One study by the author of this book demonstrated that *both* good teachers and bad ones knew equally well what a good teaching situation *ought* to be like![1] Knowing is certainly important to teaching but it is clear that good teaching involves much more.

THE "COMPETENCIES" APPROACH TO TEACHING[2]

The second approach to defining good teaching has been in terms of teacher "competencies." The thinking goes something like this: If we know what the expert teachers do, or are like, then we can teach the beginners to be like that. This is a straightforward, uncomplicated approach to the problem and seems logically sound. The idea has produced great quantities of research into the traits of good teachers and their methods.

RESEARCH ON SPECIFIC COMPETENCIES

This has provided us with long lists of competencies supposedly characteristic of good teachers. In the beginning these lists were quite simple. Since, however, what people do is always related to the situations they are in, every situation calls for a different behavior and the more situations the researchers examine, the longer the lists of competencies have become. Here for example, is a list made by a conference of "superior teachers" in 1962:

A good teacher should:

> Know his subject
> Know much about related subjects
> Be adaptable to new knowledge
> Understand the process of becoming
> Recognize individual differences
> Be a good communicator

[1] A. W. Combs and D. W. Soper, "The Helping Relationship as Described by 'Good' and 'Poor' Teachers," *J. Teacher Ed.*, 1963, **14**, 64–68.

[2] Much of the material in this and the succeeding chapter has been adapted from an article by the author first published in *Educational Leadership*: A. W. Combs, "The Personal Approach to Good Teaching," *Ed. Leadership*, 1964, **21**, 369–378.

Develop an inquiring mind
Be available
Be committed
Be enthusiastic
Have a sense of humor
Have humility
Cherish his own individuality
Have convictions
Be sincere and honest
Act with integrity
Show tolerance and understanding
Be caring
Have compassion
Have courage
Have personal security
Be creative
Be versatile
Be willing to try
Be adaptable
Believe in God

This is but a short list. There are much longer ones!

These first attempts to describe specifically the competencies of good teachers yielded few useful results. In 1929 the American Association of School Administrators commissioned a team to review the research on the problem, hoping to find some guidelines to help them make the practical decisions about teacher quality necessary in carrying on their jobs. Sadly, the team was forced to report that there is no specific trait or method exclusively associated with good teaching.[3]

RESEARCH ON GENERAL COMPETENCIES

Some investigators have thought better discriminations might result from studying the general, rather than the specific, traits or methods of good teachers. Approaching the problem in this way, they have been able to find fairly stable distinctions in such general terms as good teachers are "considerate" or "child-centered" or "concerned about structure." The most significant of these is a study by Marie Hughes[4]

[3] W. J. Ellena, M. Stevenson, and H. V. Webb, *Who's a Good Teacher?* (Washington, D. C.: American Association of School Administrators, N.E.A., 1961).

[4] Marie M. Hughes, *Development of the Means for Assessing the Quality of Teaching in Elementary Schools.* Report of Research, Cooperative Research Program, Project No. 353 (Washington, D. C.: U. S. Office of Education, 1959).

under a grant from the United States Office of Education, Cooperative Research Program. Dr. Hughes developed an exhaustive system for analyzing teacher behavior and applied this system to time-sample observations of teachers in the classroom. She was able to demonstrate a number of general classes of behavior seemingly characteristic of good teachers. Among these were such categories as controlling, imposition, facilitating, content development, response, and positive or negative affectivity. Similar attempts to analyze teacher behavior have been carried out by Flanders,[5] Smith,[6] Bowers,[7] Filson,[8] and Medley.[9] These examinations of the more general aspects of effective teaching have been somewhat more successful in discriminating between good and poor teaching than research on specific behavior or methods. But they still do not provide us with the definitive distinctions needed by the profession. Good teaching, it is clear, is not a direct function of general traits or methods. Summing up the situation, a noted educator has concluded, "It is commonplace but not very flattering to this commentator, to deplore the fact that more than half a century of research effort has not yielded meaningful, measurable criteria around which the majority of the nation's educators can rally."[10]

SOME PRACTICAL DIFFICULTIES OF THE "COMPETENCIES" APPROACH

The attempt to develop a teacher-education program based upon the "competencies" approach runs into some very knotty problems. In the first place, it is a fallacy to assume that the methods of the experts

[5] N. A. Flanders, *Teacher Influence, Pupil Attitudes and Achievement: Studies in Interaction Analysis.* Final Report, Cooperative Research Program, Project No. 397 (Washington, D. C.: U. S. Office of Education, 1960).

[6] Othanel Smith, "A Concept of Teaching," in *Language and Concepts in Education* (Chicago: Rand McNally, 1961).

[7] N. D. Bowers and R. S. Soar, *Studies in Human Relations in the Teaching Learning Process.* Final Report, Cooperative Research Program, Project No. 469 (Washington, D. C.: U. S. Office of Education, 1961).

[8] T. N. Filson, "Factors Influencing the Level of Dependence in the Classroom," Unpublished Ph.D. Thesis (Minneapolis: Univ. of Minnesota, 1957).

[9] Donald M. Medley and Harold E. Mitzel, "A Technique for Measuring Classroom Behavior," *J. Ed. Psych.* 1958, **49**, 86–92.

[10] N. Fattu, "A Profession Seeks to Guarantee the Competence of Its Members," *New Horizons in Teacher Education,* Report of the National Commission on Teacher Education and Professional Standards (Washington, D. C.: N. E. A., 1964).

Good teaching is not a direct function of general traits or methods

either can or should be taught directly to beginners. It is seldom that we can determine what should be for the beginner by examining what the expert does well. I learned this some years ago when I was responsible for teaching failing university students more effective methods of study. At first glance it would seem logical to teach the failing students the study habits of successful ones. Such an approach to curriculum construction, however, is disastrous! When one examines the study habits of successful students, one is likely to find that they study most whimsically. They operate without plan, go to the movies often, indulge in all sorts of extracurricular activities, and generally behave in ways that would be suicidal for students teetering on the brink of failure. It simply does not follow that what is good for the expert is good for the novice too! Nor is it true that the way to become expert is to do what the expert does.

Some of the methods used by the expert can only be used *because* he is expert. Many experienced teachers have learned to deal with most classroom disturbances by ignoring them. But beginners cannot ignore them! The expert is able to ignore matters precisely because he *is* expert. Some methods cannot even be comprehended without adequate prior experience. One must grow to achieve them. The attempt to use them without understanding may only serve to turn the young teacher loose in the blackboard jungle to fight for his life with inappropriate weapons.

The creation of long lists of competencies is likely to be deeply discouraging and disillusioning to the young teacher for another reason. Evaluations of "goodness" or "badness" become attached to methods, and students thereafter are expected to judge their adequacy in these terms. The net effect is to set such impossible goals of excellence that no one can ever hope to reach them. I recall the reaction of a group of young teachers I worked with some years ago when one of the members of the group brought in a survey he had found in the literature—a list of "1,000 Things a Good Teacher Should Do." Consideration of the list by this group of already harassed students produced nothing but frustration, anger, and despair. "Do teachers have to be everything?" they cried. "We just can't do all that!"

Discouraging and disillusioning as the "competencies" approach is for the young teacher, it has equally unhappy effects on the older ones. A vast complex of competencies, all of which are demanded as criteria for good teaching, leaves the individual defenseless before criticism.

No matter what he does well, it is never enough! There is always so much more that he might have done, or should have done, that he can rarely find pleasure or satisfaction in his accomplishments. Add to this the fact that many of the competencies demanded do not fit the particular personality, and so could probably never be achieved anyhow, and the defeat of the individual becomes almost inevitable. In time, the feeling of inadequacy produced by continual failure to meet impossible goals undermines professional pride and is likely to produce a guilt-ridden teacher suffering from a secret feeling of being "too little and too late." It should not be surprising if after years of this kind of experience the will to try shrivels and dies.

To use particular competencies as a measure of good teaching irrespective of personalities, situations, or purposes leads us to the ridiculous conclusion that some of the people who taught us most were poor teachers. When I hear young teachers-in-training remark, "Oh, he is a lousy teacher but you sure learn a lot," I am forced to conclude that the determination of the goodness of teaching on the basis of competencies is highly questionable.

THE PERSONAL CHARACTER OF GOOD TEACHING

THE TEACHER AS A PERSON

As we have seen, research on competencies has been unable to isolate any common trait or practice of good teachers. But this unanimous failure in itself demonstrates an important fact: a good teacher is primarily a unique personality. If good teachers are unique individuals, we can predict from the start that the attempt to find *common uniqueness* would be unlikely to get results.

A good teacher is first and foremost *a person,* and this fact is the most important and determining thing about him. He has competence, to be sure, but not a common set of competencies like anyone else. Some years ago, I visited a well-known demonstration school. Each classroom had a carefully picked teacher. Visiting the rooms in this school with the principal one day, I was much impressed with the beautiful work that many of the students had produced. Classroom after classroom was charmingly and artistically decorated with the children's productions: artwork, science demonstrations, biological specimens, collections of all sorts and descriptions. After five or six

A good teacher is a unique personality
Finding common uniqueness gets no results

such rooms we walked into another so different from the others as to be almost a shock. This room was nearly bare of the materials we had seen in the others. Instead, in this class the teacher sat in the middle of a group of children holding a quiet discussion. Leaving the room with the principal, I remarked on this fact and I was struck by the principal's reply. "Yes," she said, "and you know, I believe that is perhaps my very best teacher. She is not like the others. You can see that. But she gives those children something special. What that girl can do to help children explore an idea is simply out of this world!" Here was a teacher making full and effective use of herself in her own special ways. Fortunately, she had a principal who recognized her genius. It is probable that many a less understanding person would have condemned her for her "obvious inadequacies" as compared to other teachers in the same building.

The personal character of good teaching can be documented by almost any of us from our own experience. If one thinks back to his own school days, one will probably remember that the good teachers one has had in one's lifetime did not all behave alike or even with great similarity. Rather, each stands out as a person, an individual, some for one reason, some for another. Each had his own peculiar methods, values, and techniques. Good teaching is like that, an intensely personal thing.

THE UNIQUENESS OF METHODS

Apparently, there can be no such thing as a "good" or "bad" method of teaching. The terms "good" and "bad" can be applied to results, outcomes, purposes, or ends. The methods we use to achieve these ends, however, only derive their value from the goals and purposes for which they are used. The good teacher is not one who behaves in a given way. He is an artist, skillful in producing a desirable result. The result may be considered "good" or "bad," but not the method. Some years ago I visited an elementary school in a very tough neighborhood. I have rarely seen a principal with better rapport with his students or his faculty. While sitting in the principal's office, however, I noticed a paddle on the wall above his desk. Noting my attention to his paddle, the principal pointed out with some pride that the paddle was bolted to the wall, as indeed it was. He informed me, however, that it had not always been so. This man's predecessor had

had his collarbone broken when he was thrown down the stairs by his students. When this principal came to the job, the school board gave him one year to "clean it up or get out!" "Those were tough years," he told me. "You know, I had to lick them before I could love them." Is paddling a good method of dealing with children? As a psychologist, I cannot condone it, but when I ask myself what I would have done in this man's predicament, I frankly do not know. Maybe I would have done what he did. Whatever any of us decides he *might* do, the fact remains that this man is a good principal today in a well-run school. He did what it seemed to him he needed to do with the children he had and in the situation he was confronted with to achieve the purposes he had in mind.

The description of methods or competencies as "good" or "bad" in themselves is much too simple. The methods we use must take into account people, situations, and purposes. The same criteria cannot be applied equally to the beautiful school in the wealthy suburbs and the dingy school in the slum. Though its methods may seem less enlightened, the school in the slum could be doing a better job, given its particular problems and situations, than the wealthy school in the suburbs. The development of students and the growth of intelligence and personality are the goals we seek, and whether these are being achieved or not cannot be judged from a study of the methods employed in the achievement of such ends.

THE "SELF AS INSTRUMENT" CONCEPT

The shift in our thinking from a mechanistic to a personal view of teaching is by no means confined to our profession alone. In fact, most other professions dealing with human problems have preceded us in this direction. The effective professional worker is no longer regarded as a technician applying methods in a more or less mechanical fashion the way he has been taught. We now see him as an intelligent human being using himself, his knowledge, and the resources at hand to solve the problems for which he is responsible. He is a person who has learned to use himself as an effective instrument. In medicine, this principle finds expression in the "problems approach" to training. In social work, it is found in the concept of supervision. Modern nursing has adopted a human relations approach to patient care. Counseling and psychotherapy stress the philosophy of the counselor and the importance of his own personal therapy. These professions do not seek the production of automatons. They want creative, thinking human beings able to use themselves as refined and trustworthy instruments for dealing with complex problems.

If we adapt this "self as instrument" concept of the professional worker to teaching, it means that teacher-education programs must concern themselves with persons rather than competencies. It means that the individualization of instruction we have sought for the public schools must be applied to these programs as well. It calls for the production of creative individuals, capable of shifting and changing to meet the demands and opportunities afforded in daily tasks. Such a teacher will not behave in a set way. His behavior will change from moment to moment, from day to day, adjusting continually and smoothly to the needs of his students, the situations he is in, the purposes he seeks to fulfill, and the methods and materials at his command.

The good teacher is no carbon copy but possesses something intensely and personally his own. Artists sometimes call this "the discovery of one's personal idiom." The good teacher has found ways of using himself, his talents, and his surroundings in a fashion that aids both his students and himself to achieve satisfaction—their own and society's too. We may define the effective teacher formally as *a unique human being who has learned to use himself effectively and efficiently to carry out his own and society's purposes in the education of others.*

How shall a teacher-education program produce such a person? To answer this question we need a frame of reference about the nature of behavior and learning on which to base our thinking and a more precise look at the "self as instrument" concept of good teaching.

2

A Perceptual View of Effective Teaching

*I*F THE "SELF AS INSTRUMENT" CONCEPT of the professional worker is valid, then teacher education must result in the production of that kind of self. To provide the guidelines for such a program we need to know 1) the nature of the self, 2) how it develops, 3) how it may be changed, and 4) what a good teaching self is like; we need a "self" psychology on which to base our operations. Modern humanistic psychology supplies us with just such kinds of understanding. This way of looking at people and their behavior is quite different from the psychology most of today's teacher educators grew up with.

Present-day teacher education is still deeply influenced by the stimulus-response (S-R) approach to human behavior characteristic of American psychology for fifty years. When it first appeared on the scene many educators embraced it wholeheartedly, hoping it might provide the basis for a scientific approach to problems of teaching and learning. But this hope has given way to disappointment as it has become clear that so mechanistic a view of psychology cannot supply the answers we need. As American education has become increasingly child- or student-centered, the approach to human behavior characteristic of stimulus-response psychology has proven less and less adequate in enabling teachers to carry out their tasks. A whole new practice has arisen calling for new theoretical concepts, new understandings, and new directions.

Theory and practice in human experience do not always develop concurrently. Rather, progress seems to be characterized by a kind of leap-frog operation in which first one, then the other, steps into the lead, each building on past achievements. Sometimes theory moves ahead of practice, sometimes practice outruns theory. So it is in the relationship between psychology and teaching.

THIRD FORCE PSYCHOLOGY

THE EMERGENCE OF THIRD FORCE PSYCHOLOGY

Three great movements have characterized American psychology in the past seventy years. The earliest of these was stimulus-response psychology, which originally grew out of attempts to apply the new techniques of the physical sciences to problems of human behavior. Its greatest effect upon education in particular came in the 1920's and 1930's: it was then that educational psychology came into being and that the ideas of stimulus-response psychology began to be applied to educational problems. For a while the application of these ideas to teaching-learning problems proved helpful and stimulating. But S-R psychology was not an unmixed blessing; its essentially mechanistic character served to lead the profession down some primrose paths from which many are still unable to turn. For more than a generation best teaching practice has outrun the contributions of stimulus-response psychology as teachers everywhere have discovered more humanistic approaches to learning.

Following World War I, American psychology was caught up in a second great movement, largely stimulated by Freud and his followers. The effect of this psychoanalytic movement was to turn the attention of many psychologists to problems of human behavior outside the laboratory, and they began to search for the causes of behavior in the life history of the individual. This was really an extension of the S-R approach: it included not just immediate stimuli, but the whole gamut of experiences to which a person had been subjected in his lifetime. Looking at man in this way provided useful clues for dealing with many of our educational problems. It still does, but the S-R and psychoanalytic psychological viewpoints are objective, descriptive ways of looking at behavior and lead to mechanistic or manipulative ways of working with people which are often not acceptable in modern practice. Over the years American education has moved increasingly toward a more humanistic philosophy which finds expression in practices designed to facilitate and assist learning rather than to control and direct it. We have outrun traditional psychologies; modern educational thought and practice calls for new understandings of behavior more adequate to deal with our current problems. We need a new psychology to help us with these matters.

Fortunately that psychology is at hand. A new Third Force in American psychology has appeared on the scene during the last twenty years. Psychologists involved in this movement are called by many names. In the group may be found personalists, humanists, self psychologists, phenomenologists, perceptual psychologists, transactionalists, existentialists, and a number of others. All have in common a deep concern with questions of man's being and becoming. They take a view of behavior that is highly consistent with the experience of superior teachers: it is a point of view that sees people as growing, dynamic organisms. It regards human beings not as things to be made or molded but as unique events in the process of becoming. The impact of this new psychology is being felt everywhere in those professions having to do with the growth, development, and welfare of people. It has tremendous importance for education. In particular, it provides the framework for a "self as instrument" approach to teacher education.

THREE BASIC PRINCIPLES OF PERCEPTUAL PSYCHOLOGY

For those readers not familiar with the perceptual-existential approach to psychology, let us briefly review three of its basic principles. While a high degree of similarity exists in the basic points of view of Third Force psychologists, it should be understood that there are also important differences among them. The principles presented below are drawn from my own brand of Third Force psychology. They would probably be acceptable to many other Third Force psychologists, but not to all of them. For the reader who would like to explore these concepts more deeply, a selected list of references has been included at the end of this chapter.

The Perceptual Basis of Behavior. The basic concept of perceptual psychology is that all behavior of a person is the direct result of his field of perceptions at the moment of his behaving. More specifically, his behavior at any instant is the result of 1) how he sees himself, 2) how he sees the situations in which he is involved, and 3) the interrelations of these two. When I see myself as a lecturer, standing in front of an audience, I behave like a lecturer. My audience, on the other hand, seeing themselves as an audience, behaves like an audience. Each of us behaves in terms of what seems to him to be appropriate for the kind of person he sees himself to be in the situation he is in at that moment. The immediate causes of behavior are to be found in the perceptions existing for the behaver at the moment of acting. This seems like a simple, acceptable notion that fits very closely with our own experience.

Perhaps it is precisely because it fits so closely and comfortably that it is often overlooked. One's own perceptions of events seem so "right" and so certain that one is quite likely to jump to the conclusion that the way one sees things is the way things are. Our own percep- *Russell!* tions have such a feeling of reality that when others do not see things in a similar fashion we are likely to jump to either of two conclusions: They are frightfully stupid for not seeing correctly, or else they are perversely trying to annoy and confound us! It is probable that such failure to understand how things seem to other people is the most persistent source of difficulties in human relationships. To understand human behavior, the perceptual psychologist says, it is necessary to understand the behaver's perceptual world, how things seem from his point of view.

This calls for a different understanding of what the "facts" are that we need in order to deal with human behavior: It is not the external facts which are important in understanding behavior, but the meaning of the facts to the behaver. To change another person's behavior it is necessary somehow to modify his beliefs or perceptions. When he sees things differently, he will behave differently.

This change in our frame of reference for understanding people brings about a thorough revision of our thinking about many problems of human behavior and interaction, and many psychologists regard it as one of the great break-throughs of the social sciences. Perceptual psychology has already had profound effects on other professions like social work, counseling, and psychotherapy. It is having equally profound effects on the work of many teachers. The ideas seem particularly applicable to the problems of education but nowhere more so than in the production of effective teachers.

For several generations we have been preoccupied with the "competencies" approach to teacher education with its emphasis upon teaching teachers how they *ought* to behave. Perceptual psychology,

why are we should not be concerned with how people ought to behave.

however, tells us that behavior is only a symptom, the surface manifestation of what is going on within the individual. To attack
behavior directly is to deal with symptoms rather than causes, and a
symptomatic approach to human behavior is no more likely to be
permanently effective than a symptomatic approach to health. Teaching people to behave differently at one time cannot be counted upon to
affect their behavior at another. Perhaps this explains why so much
of what we teach in teacher-preparation programs is slow to find its
way into actual practice of the new teacher in the classroom.

If behavior is a function of perception, it follows that teacher
education must concern itself with the inner life of its students.
Simple exposure to subject matter is not enough. The maturation of
an effective professional worker requires changes in the student's perceptions—his feelings, attitudes, and beliefs and his understandings of
himself and his world. This is no easy matter, for what lies inside
the individual is not open to direct manipulation and control. It is
unlikely to change except with the active involvement of the student
in the process.

The Self-Concept and Behavior. Of all the perceptions existing for
an individual, none are so important as those he has about himself.
Each of us has thousands of ways in which he sees himself and each
of these has more or less importance in a given personal economy. I
may see myself as a man, husband, father, psychologist, professor, as
middle-aged, a resident of Florida, an American, able to swim but not
to play polo, adequate to teach personality theory but not statistics,
and so on. These and thousands of others make up the peculiar
organization which seems to me to be my "very self." It is this organization of ways of seeing self that the modern psychologist calls the
self-concept. It represents the most important single influence affecting an individual's behavior.

The individual's self is the center of his world, the point of origin
for all behavior. What he believes about himself affects every aspect
of his life. We now know that many academic deficiencies can be
traced to unfortunate concepts of self. For example, most children
who come to reading clinics do not come because they have anything
wrong with their eyes. The children who come to the reading clinic
are, almost without exception, unable to read because they *believe* they

cannot read. That is to say, they have developed *concepts of them-selves* as people who cannot read. They are prisoners of their own unfortunate self-perceptions. Similar deficiencies in other subjects can be traced to children's ideas about themselves as unable to spell, unable to write, unable to do algebra, or whatever. In adulthood people may suffer from feelings of being unable to make a speech, dance, or do arithmetic. Millions of people are victims of the beliefs they hold about themselves.

The effect of the self-concept extends far beyond the matter of skills, however. We now know that even an individual's adjustment or maladjustment is likely to depend on the ways in which he perceives himself. The psychotherapist knows that the maladjusted persons with whom he works are people who characteristically see themselves as unliked, unwanted, unacceptable, unable. On the other hand, ade-quate, effective, efficient, self-actualizing, well-adjusted citizens are persons whose self-concepts are highly positive. They perceive them-selves to be persons who are liked, wanted, acceptable, able. They see themselves as belonging, responsible, effective personalities, and because they see themselves so, they behave so. Teachers, too, are affected by the adequacy of their self-concepts.

The self-concept is not something you are born with. It is some-thing each of us learns as a consequence of his experience with those who surround him in the process of his growing up. We *learn* that we are men or women, able or unable, acceptable or unacceptable, liked or unliked, depending upon the kinds of experiences we have had in the process of growing up. Once established, the concepts we have of ourselves continue to affect our behavior, perhaps even for life.

All this means that teacher education must be deeply concerned about the developing self of the fledgling teacher. How a teacher behaves after he leaves the portals of his college will be very largely determined by how he has learned to see himself and his relationships to his students, his subject matter, and to the profession of teaching itself. Teacher education must thus become as student-centered as we have hoped the teachers we are currently producing would be in their own classrooms. To provide a frame of reference for the construction of its curriculum it also needs the most accurate understanding of the kinds of self-perceptions associated with effective teaching. We will return to this point later in this chapter.

The Basic Need for Personal Adequacy. The most important thing about man is his existence, the fact of his being and becoming. Modern psychology sees man as engaged in a continuous striving for self-fulfillment. In this process each of us seeks by every means he can to be "enough," not just for the present but for the future as well. The basic need for personal adequacy thus includes both striving for self-maintenance and for self-enhancement. It is not the physical self each of us seeks to maintain, however. It is the self of which we are aware, our *self-concepts,* we seek fulfillment for. Even behaviors which at first glance seem to be self-destructive turn out to be self-maintaining or enhancing when they are seen from the point of view of the individual. So it is that the hero may give himself up to certain death rather than see himself as a coward or a traitor to his fellows. In our own experiences we often place our physical selves in jeopardy for the sake of enhancing our concepts of self. For example, we drive too fast, eat too much, work too hard, even when we know better.

The need for adequacy is the fundamental motivation of every human being from conception to death. It provides the drive toward health and mobilization of the body's resources to resist the attacks of disease. And it causes the client in psychotherapy to move toward better adjustment and personal development when he is helped by the therapist to remove the blocks that lie in the path of his recovery. The drive toward health does not have to be learned; it is a characteristic of life itself and provides the motive power for every human act.

This drive has tremendous implications for education. Its existence means it is not necessary to motivate people—a problem we have often struggled with. Everyone is *always motivated* to be and become as adequate as he can be in the situations as he sees them. Students may not be motivated as their teachers would like, but they are always motivated in terms of their own basic need.

Knowledge of this innate drive changes the whole structure of the educative process from that which our ancestors felt was essential. If people are always motivated to become as adequate as they can, they are seeking the same goals for themselves that their teachers ought to be seeking for them! The task of the teacher is not one of prescribing, making, molding, forcing, coercing, coaxing, or cajoling; it is one of ministering to a process already in being. The role required of the teacher is that of facilitator, encourager, helper, assister, colleague, and friend of his students.

In the pages that follow I have attempted to point out some of the implications that these principles of perceptual psychology have for teacher-education practices. Before we turn to that question, however, we need to look more closely at the "self as instrument" concept of teaching. If the effective use of self as instrument is to become the goal of teacher education, we need to define more precisely what kind of self that is.

THE HELPING RELATIONSHIP

In recent years a number of psychologists have been examining the nature of the helping relationship.[1] One of the most interesting of their findings is that helping relationships, wherever they are found, seem to have a high degree of similarity. These kinds of relationships are to be found in many places and in many kinds of settings created by many different kinds of people. Wherever they are found, however, they seem to have certain common characteristics. That is true in the classroom, the counseling office, in psychotherapy, or in the relations between teachers and supervisors, supervisors and principals, or administrators and staff.

In one study a number of psychotherapists from different schools of thought were asked by Fiedler[2] to describe what they considered to be the elements of an ideal therapeutic relationship. He found that experienced therapists from different schools of thought were in greater agreement about the nature of the helping relationship than were beginning and expert therapists of the same school. Apparently, no matter what the school of thought from which these therapists began their work, as they grew more experienced they came to see the helping relationship in highly similar terms. Even more surprising, when Fiedler asked "the man in the street" to describe the nature of a good helping relationship, he found that the ordinary citizen described it about as well as the experts! It would appear from this that there is such a thing as a "good" human relationship, and that all of us, professional or not, as a consequence of our experience are able more or less explicitly to recognize it when we meet it.

[1] C. R. Rogers, "The Characteristics of a Helping Relationship," *Personnel and Guidance J.*, 1958, **37**, 6–16.
[2] F. E. Fiedler, "The Concept of an Ideal Therapeutic Relationship," *J. Consult. Psych.*, 1950, **14**, 239–245.

Several years ago I became intrigued with these results. I wondered if the helping relationship as seen by good teachers would agree with the relationship as seen by expert psychotherapists. Accordingly, one of my colleagues and I applied Fiedler's helping relationship Q-sort to a group of superior teachers in a university laboratory school. Sure enough, the good teachers were in close agreement with the expert therapists about what a helping relationship ought to be like.[3] We next applied this instrument to two groups of "very good" and "very poor" teachers selected for us by students and supervisors.[4] We expected to find considerable differences, but quite the contrary, we found poor teachers could describe the good helping relationship just as well as the good ones. Apparently everyone knows what a good helping relationship *ought* to be like even if he cannot produce it.

Psychologists who have been investigating the nature of the helping relationship are unable to define it on the basis of specific things which helpers *do*. They can, however, discriminate between good helpers and poor helpers on the basis of their perceptions. When we look at the question of what helpers do, we find that they behave in hundreds of diverse ways, among which there seems to be no common characteristic. When, however, we look at the perceptual organization of helpers we begin to find important differences between good helpers and the poor ones. For example, it has been found that helpers can be distinguished from nonhelpers on the basis of their attitudes, feelings, purposes, and their conceptions of themselves and others.[5] Since good teaching is also a kind of helping relationship, these findings suggest again the importance of a perceptual approach to teacher-education programs.

THE PERCEPTUAL VIEW OF EFFECTIVE TEACHING

The need to take a perceptual view of teacher education has already been suggested by a number of other writers.[6,7,8,9,10,11] It is the basic

---

[3] D. W. Soper and A. W. Combs, "The Helping Relationship As Seen by Teachers and Therapists," *J. Consult. Psych.*, 1962, **26**, 288.

[4] A. W. Combs and D. W. Soper, "The Helping Relationship As Described by 'Good' and 'Poor' Teachers," *J. Teacher Ed.*, 1963, **14**, 64–68.

[5] A. W. Combs and D. W. Soper, "Perceptual Organization of Effective Counselors," *J. Counsel. Psych.*, 1963, **10**, No. 3, 222–226.

[6] W. R. Dixon and W. C. Morse, "The Prediction of Teaching Performance: Empathic Potential," *J. Teacher Ed.*, 1961, **12**, 322–329.

thesis of this book. Whether an individual will be an effective teacher depends upon the nature of his private world of perceptions. It follows that the perceptual world of the student must be a matter of vital concern to teacher-education programs.

If teacher education is to be concerned with changing student perceptions, we need clear definitions of what the perceptual organizations of effective teachers are like. We need a tremendous research effort to explore that question with the greatest possible speed. This is coming. Already there is a quickening of interest in these matters, and it is probable that we shall have detailed experimental evidence in considerable quantities within the next four or five years. We do not need to wait, however, for there is already evidence enough to start us thinking in new directions, designing new techniques, and planning for the research we need. At present we have the following sources of information to draw upon for defining the probable dimensions of good teaching in perceptual terms:

1. Perceptual psychological theory, especially that having to do with the nature of the self and fully functioning behavior;
2. Research on the perceptions of good practitioners in other helping professions;
3. The research already existing in our profession;
4. The experiences accumulated by thousands of teachers engaged in day-to-day "action research" in the classroom.

For nearly five years at the University of Florida we have been wrestling with the question, "What kinds of perceptions do 'good' professional workers have?" Our studies began with a year-long seminar devoted to the question in 1960. Out of this study we developed a series of hypotheses which we thought were probably char-

[7] Margaret Lindsey, *New Horizons for the Teaching Profession* (Washington, D. C.: National Commission on Teacher Education and Professional Standards, N. E. A., 1961).

[8] W. W. Lynch, "Person Perception: Its Role in Teaching," *Indiana Univ. School of Ed. Bull.*, 1961, **37**, 1–37.

[9] P. E. McClendon, "Teacher Perception and Working Climate," *Ed. Leadership*, 1962, **20**, 104–109.

[10] C. P. Ramsey, "Leadership Preparation," *Ed. Leadership*, 1962, **20**, 151–154.

[11] D. G. Ryans, *Characteristics of Teachers* (Washington, D. C.: American Council on Education, 1960).

acteristic of good professional workers.[12]   Since then we have been engaged in a series of researches designed to measure whether our beliefs about good professional workers' perceptions were really so. To this date we have been able to test our hypotheses on counselors,[13] Episcopal priests[14] and teachers.[15]   In each instance our hypotheses have been verified to an extent even we were unprepared to expect.

As a consequence of these studies we have come to believe that the following major areas are crucial in the perceptual organization of a good teacher:

1. Rich, extensive, and available perceptions about his subject field.
2. Accurate perceptions about what people are like.
3. Perceptions of self leading to adequacy.
4. Accurate perceptions about the purpose and process of learning.
5. Personal perceptions about appropriate methods for carrying out his purposes.

We now examine these in more detail.

THE GOOD TEACHER IS WELL INFORMED

The good teacher is not stupid. He has a rich, extensive, and available field of perceptions about the subject matter for which he is responsible. This is the aspect of teacher education upon which everybody agrees: Teachers should be knowledgeable people. It is also the aspect with which teacher education has traditionally been most successful. What is often not understood by many critics of modern education is that teachers rarely fail because of lack of knowledge of subject matter. When they fail it is almost always because they have been unable to transmit what they know so that it makes a difference to their students.

It should be clearly understood that the perceptual view of teacher education considers this "knowing" phase to be of first-rank, though

---

[12] A. W. Combs, "A Perceptual View of the Nature of 'Helpers' in Personality Theory and Counseling Practice," *Papers of Annual Conference on Personality Theory and Counseling Practice*, 1961, 53–58.

[13] A. W. Combs and D. W. Soper, "Perceptual Organization of Effective Counselors," *J. Counsel. Psych.*, 1963, **10**, No. 3, 222–226.

[14] John A. Benton, "Perceptual Characteristics of Episcopal Pastors," Unpublished Ed.D. Dissertation (Gainesville: Univ. of Florida, 1964).

[15] C. T. Gooding, "An Observational Analysis of the Perceptual Organization of Effective Teachers," Unpublished Ed.D. Dissertation (Gainesville: Univ. of Florida, 1964).

not exclusive, importance in the professional training of teachers. But generally speaking, we have done much better with this phase of teacher education than with any other. Therefore, if the matter seems to be given less emphasis in this book than other aspects of teacher education, this is not because it is less important, but only because it is less in need of attention. "It is the squeaky wheel that gets the grease."

ACCURATE PERCEPTIONS ABOUT PEOPLE AND THEIR BEHAVIOR

Teaching is a human relationship. To behave effectively good teachers must possess the most accurate understandings about people and their behavior available in our time. Each of us can only behave in terms of what he believes is so. What a teacher believes, therefore, about the nature of his students will have a most important effect on how he behaves toward them. If a teacher believes his students have the capacity to learn, he will behave quite differently from the teacher who has serious doubts about the capacities of his charges. The teacher who believes his students can learn begins his task with hope and assurance that both he and his students may be successful. He can place confidence and trust in his students and be certain that if he is successful in facilitating and encouraging the learning process they can, they *will* learn. The teacher, on the other hand, who does not believe his students are capable approaches his task with two strikes against him. If you do not believe that children can learn, it is surely not safe to trust them.

Teachers need a clear and consistent frame of reference about people and their behavior to serve as a guide in dealing with them. This need not be a formal psychology represented by a particular school of thought, but it must be as accurate and true-to-life as possible. False beliefs about the nature of people can only result in the selection of inappropriate ways of dealing with them. The good teacher's psychology must be more than accurate, however. It must also be a point of view to which the teacher is deeply committed, for without personal involvement no point of view has any significant effect upon behavior. It is a personal psychology which the good teacher needs, derived from accurate observations and given consistency and meaning by personal exploration and discovery. A prime function of the teacher-preparation program must be to assist its students in the development of such a frame of reference for their future behavior.

PERCEPTIONS ABOUT THE SELF

The behavior of a teacher, like that of everyone else, is a function of his concepts of self. Teachers who believe they are able will try. Teachers who do not think they are able will avoid responsibilities. Teachers who feel they are liked by their students will behave quite differently from those who feel they are unliked. Teachers who feel they are acceptable to the administration can behave quite differently from those who have serious doubts about their acceptability. Teachers who feel their profession has dignity and integrity can themselves behave with dignity and integrity. Teachers who have grave doubts about the importance and value of their profession may behave apologetically or overly aggressively with their students and with their colleagues.

It is apparent that if the self-concepts a person holds about himself are as important in determining behavior as modern psychology suggests, then teacher educators must be deeply concerned with the kinds of self-concepts teachers in training are developing. This is comparatively new ground for the teacher-education program. Teaching subject matter has always been a recognized task. Even teaching psychology has long been accepted as a responsibility. But few teacher educators so far have given much thought to incorporating good self-concept development in their programs. A "self as instrument" approach to teacher education must assign this question a high priority. We need to seek from research workers much more information about the kinds of self-perceptions characteristic of good teachers. And we need to examine teacher-education curricula and practices with an eye to their effects upon the self-concepts of students.

PERCEPTIONS ABOUT THE PURPOSES AND PROCESS OF LEARNING

Behavior always has direction. Whatever we do is always determined by the purposes we have in mind at the time of our behaving or misbehaving. What teachers perceive to be their own and society's purposes makes a great deal of difference in their behavior. The teacher who believes that schools exist only for the able and that "it is a waste of time to fool with the poorer students," behaves quite differently from the teacher who perceives society's purpose as helping all children become the best they can. Similarly, what teachers believe about how students learn will markedly affect their behavior. One teacher, believing children must be molded, teaches loyalty to country by carefully censoring what students read and hear about democracy and Communism. Another teacher, believing children learn best when confronted with all kinds of evidence, takes a different tack in teaching his class.

Teachers work in the midst of purposes: the nation's, the local community's, the administration's, the parents', the children's, and their own. Whether any of these ever achieve fulfillment will depend upon the particular resolution the teacher makes in his own personal economy with respect to all these purposes. A major task of the teacher-education program must be to help the student explore these purposes and to arrive at his own understanding of them in so personal a way that they become a part of his very being.

APPROPRIATE METHODS OF TEACHING

As we have already suggested, the methods teachers use must fit the kinds of people they are. An effective teacher must have a stock of methods he may call upon as needed to carry out his teaching duties. These may vary widely from teacher to teacher and even from moment to moment. But whatever their nature they must fit the situations and purposes of the teacher and be appropriate for the students with whom they are used.

The teaching of methods has long been regarded as a prime function of teacher education. Indeed, there are some who have complained of a preoccupation with them. The "self as instrument" concept of professional training, however, places a different emphasis on the matter. The teacher-education program must help each student find the methods best suited to him, to his purposes, his task, and the peculiar populations and problems with which he must deal on the job. This is not so much a matter of *teaching* methods as one of helping students to *discover* methods. It is a question of finding the methods right for the teacher rather than right for teaching.

In the chapters to follow I have tried to explore more fully the implications of perceptual psychology for each of the five areas characteristic of effective professional workers.

SUGGESTED SUPPLEMENTARY READING IN THIRD FORCE PSYCHOLOGY

ALLPORT, GORDON. *Becoming* (New Haven, Conn.: Yale Univ. Press, 1955).

BILLS, R. E. *About People and Teaching* (Lexington: Bureau of School Service, Univ. of Kentucky, 1955).

COMBS, A. W., ed. *Perceiving, Behaving, Becoming: A New Focus for Education*, 1962 ASCD Yearbook (Washington, D. C.: Association for Supervision and Curriculum Development, 1962).

COMBS, A. W. and DONALD SNYGG. *Individual Behavior* (New York: Harper, 1959).

FROMM, ERIC. *The Art of Loving* (New York: Harper, 1956).

———. *Man For Himself* (New York: Rinehart, 1947).

ITTELSON, W. H., and H. CANTRIL. *Perception, a Transactional Approach* (New York: Doubleday, 1954).

JOURARD, SYDNEY M. *Personal Adjustment* (New York: Macmillan, 1958).

KELLEY, EARL C. *Education For What Is Real* (New York: Harper, 1947).

KELLEY, EARL C. and MARIE I. RASEY. *Education and the Nature of Man* (New York: Harper, 1952).

KUENZLI, ALFRED E., ed. *The Phenomenological Problem* (New York: Harper, 1959).

LANE, HOWARD and MARY BEAUCHAMP. *Understanding Human Development* (Englewood Cliffs, N. J.: Prentice-Hall, 1959).

LECKY, P. *Self Consistency: A Theory of Personality* (New York: Island Press, 1945).

MASLOW, A. H. *Motivation and Personality* (New York: Harper, 1954).

———. *New Knowledge in Human Values* (New York: Harper, 1959).

———. *Toward a Psychology of Being* (Princeton, N. J.: Van Nostrand, 1962).

MOUSTAKAS, C. E. *The Self; Explorations in Personal Growth* (New York: Harper, 1956).

MAY, ROLLO. *Existence* (New York: Basic Books, 1958).

———, ed. *Existential Psychology* (New York: Random House, 1961).

ROGERS, CARL R. *On Becoming a Person* (Boston: Houghton Mifflin, 1961).

SULLIVAN, H. S. *Conceptions of Modern Psychiatry* (New York: Norton, 1953).

3

Creating Effective Teachers

GOOD TEACHING, WE HAVE SUGGESTED, is an intensely personal matter. It is a problem of personal discovery, of learning to use one's self as instrument. To achieve these ends the teacher-preparation curriculum must provide more than a contemplation of subject matter and teaching technique. The crucial test is in *doing* something with them.

CREATING EFFECTIVE PRACTITIONERS

For many years a misunderstanding has existed between those responsible for the subject-matter training of teachers and those responsible for the professional aspects of teacher preparation. This seems to have come about because of a confusion over purposes.

The purposes involved in producing a professional practitioner are different from those of producing a scholar. Where intentions are different, there must also be differing goals, techniques, and procedures for their realization. Failure to understand this fact is responsible for some of the friction and misunderstandings that arise between professors of education and their counterparts in the more traditional subject-matter areas.[1]

Everyone is familiar from his own behavior with the fact that there is a considerable gap between knowing and behaving. Most of us know a good deal better than we behave. Possessing knowledge is no guarantee that a person will use it. So, too, there is a difference between the scholar (knower) and practitioner (behaver). The education of the scholar is essentially directed toward content: the acquisi-

---

[1] G. K. Hodenfield and T. M. Stinnett, *The Education of Teachers* (Englewood Cliffs, N. J.: Prentice-Hall, 1961).

tion, organization, and understanding of information. The goal of the practitioner is the effective use of knowledge. For the scholar, content is crucial. For the practitioner, application is the heart of the task. It is possible for the scholar to learn his subject with little or no concern for action or for the human consequences of his understandings. The practitioner on the other hand, primarily concerned about action and human welfare, may be able to practice on occasion with little concern for content. Both the scholar and the practitioner can, of course, exist in the same skin. When they do, that is marvelous. These conditions are not synonymous, however, and the training of one does not guarantee the other. Since we cannot keep people in school for unlimited periods of time, we usually have to be content with producing people who are more or less one or the other.

The responsibility of the teacher-education program is the development of professional workers, persons who can be counted upon to act upon knowledge as well as to have it. The dynamics involved in this difference between knowing and behaving are often not well enough understood.

Because the purposes of the scholar and practitioner are different, their values, goals, and methods of operation are likely to be different too. As a consequence, communication between them often breaks down, and they pass each other like ships in the night. This kind of communication failure has often been responsible for the frictions occurring between subject-matter faculties and faculties in education. Such differences are by no means restricted to education, however. Scholars and practitioners in every discipline frequently fail to understand one another because they look through quite different glasses. This is true whether we are talking about the laboratory psychologist and the clinical psychologist, the biologist and the physician, the sociologist and the social worker, the physicist and the engineer, or the scholar and the teacher.

The ancient argument between scholar and practitioner will probably never be fully resolved. As long as people see what they do as important, they will probably continue to feel that what others do is less so. We can waste a good deal of time and energy getting embroiled in this kind of argument. We need to accept the fact that professional training *must* be different from content training and get on with the important business of producing the best practitioners we can to meet the pressing problems of our generation.

Teacher education, like education generally, has done pretty well in two of its phases. It has been quite successful in gathering information and in making information available to students. We have done this by gathering information in our libraries and in the minds of brilliant teachers. We have learned also to make this information available to other people through lectures, demonstrations, and the whole new world of audio-visual techniques. We are experts at telling people what they need to know, and we measure the success of teaching by requiring students to tell it back to us. If they do this satisfactorily, we commend them for knowing and rest content that we have taught them well. Much of educational practice never gets beyond this level of learning. But there is a third phase of the learning process essential for teacher education, with which we have not done so well. It is helping people to discover the personal meaning of information so that they *behave* differently as a result of teaching. Research has shown that both good teachers and bad know what they ought to do. Most of us are like the old farmer who, when he was asked why he was not using modern methods, replied, "Heck, I ain't farmin' now half as well as I know how!"

THE PERCEPTUAL VIEW OF EFFECTIVE LEARNING

The perceptual psychologist views learning as a personal discovery of meaning by the student, a highly personal matter involving the way he sees himself and his experience. Let us take an example to illustrate the point:

At breakfast this morning I read in the paper about "pulmonic stenosis." Now I have told this to you. Any effect on your behavior? Probably not! This bit of information is very likely as strange to you as it was to me when I read it. It has little personal meaning and so affects your behavior very little. As isolated words whose meaning you do not know, this term has little effect. Now, suppose I tell you that this is a disorder of the heart and refers to a narrowing or closing of the pulmonary artery. The same piece of information now has a little more meaning for you. You may feel vaguely uncomfortable or hope that "this doesn't happen to me!" Let us go further. Suppose I tell you that this is a disorder with which some children are born and which, if not corrected, can have most serious consequences as a child grows older. If you are a teacher and concerned with children, the same piece of information is now a little closer. As a consequence it has more effect on your behavior. You pay more attention. You listen more intently. You think about it, speculate on it. Let us now give these words a little more personal meaning. Suppose you have just heard this phrase in a letter from the mother of one of the children in your class. She writes you that her child has pulmonary stenosis and will need to be operated on in the near future. The words now have a *much* more personal bearing and produce a number of effects on behavior. Perhaps you write to the mother. You certainly discuss it with other teachers. You worry about it. You are especially nice to this child. Because the information has a more personal meaning for you, you behave much more precisely, much more certainly, with respect to it. Let us go one step further. Assume you have just been told by your doctor that you have this disorder yourself! Now, indeed, your behavior is deeply affected. All kinds of things may occur because of your new awareness!

The basic principle of learning in perceptual psychology is this: Any item of information will affect an individual's behavior only in the degree to which he has discovered its personal meaning for him. The production of effective teachers will require helping each student to explore and discover his personal meanings about subject matter, people, purposes, and learning, about methods and about himself. The source of many of our failures in teacher education, it now seems clear, is that we have not sufficiently understood that professional training must operate on these deeper, more personal, levels of learning. We have assumed that knowing and behaving are one and that the time-honored ways of teaching subject matter are appropriate for teaching people to teach as well. Our effort has been involved with teaching our students *about teaching* instead of helping them to *become teachers*. To the contrary, as we have seen, professional teacher education must be an intensely human process designed to involve the student deeply and personally.

THE NEED FOR COMMITMENT

Providing adequate opportunities for student commitment in college is not easy for two reasons: 1) We do not know how to deal with the commitment phase of learning as effectively as we know how to provide new information. Professors have been lecturing at students for generations and all of us are familiar with the techniques of telling others what is what. It is easy to do something we know how to do. It is a much more difficult thing to know how to get other people to do or to see. 2) Students and teachers alike often resist the idea of involvement because of an archaic concept of learning as a matter of taking in new information. When learning is seen solely as acquisition of knowledge, teachers become uneasy over time spent in discussion and interaction. They become impatient to push on to new ideas and concepts, and they become slaves to outlines and feel impelled to "cover the subject." The students, on their part, having been brought up by such teachers, perceive the matter in the same fashion. They too make learning synonymous with listening to experts and feel they are wasting valuable time engaging in interaction with others.

It is apparent that teacher-training curricula must go very much further in the direction of providing and supervising opportunities for commitment and involvement of their students. This will also call for a greatly increased responsibility on the part of the student for his own educational experience.[2,3] A program dependent upon encounter and involvement as great as that called for in teacher education cannot teach its students in spite of themselves. It must enlist their active involvement in at least the following ways:

Personal Involvement With Ideas. Involvement implies for some people only active, physical interaction, but people can be involved with ideas too. We need to find ways to help students participate fully in the excitement of ideas, to know the joy of taking one and running with it. Too often we have dealt with ideas as though they were sacrosanct and could not be dealt with roughly. This is too bad, for it robs scholarship of much of its excitement and pleasure. Students need to be encouraged to search out the implications of ideas, to find out what they mean, to value and glory in them! They need to understand that ideas are not just to be learned but to be wrestled with, fought with, stretched, kicked around, explored, tested, and subjected to every indignity.

[2] National Commission on Teacher Education and Professional Standards, *Changes in Teacher Education* (Washington, D. C.: N. E. A., 1963).
[3] Margaret Lindsey, *New Horizons for the Teaching Profession* (Washington, D. C.: National Commission on Teacher Education and Professional Standards, N. E. A., 1961).

Students need to be encouraged to do this not just with other people's ideas but with their own too. All the good ideas are not "out there somewhere." Indeed, the only good ideas that affect an individual's behavior are those he either has or has come to adopt as his own. The good teacher is committed. He is a thinking, feeling, believing, understanding person creatively dealing with ideas and events.

Personal Involvement in the Program. Students in a professional program should be involved as actors, not simply as spectators. They must feel a part of the process in which they are involved. To produce this feeling they must be listened to as well as talked at. They must be helped to have a feeling of belonging, to be involved in the processes which are going on—especially in the decisions regarding themselves. We cannot afford to have students in a professional college feeling about themselves as though they were no more than numbers on a computer card. They must feel that they are, in fact, important persons in their own right, participating in every aspect of program in which the faculty can find a way of interesting them.

Personal Involvement With Children. Most teacher-education programs have now become pretty thoroughly committed to the idea that students in training should be involved with children.[4] For the most part this is brought about through observations, limited forms of participation in the classroom, and finally in the internship. Since children are the raw material with which teachers must eventually work, it would appear we could profit from a great deal more involvement with children outside as well as inside the classroom. We need to find ways of involving professional students in all kinds of settings, depending upon what it is they are getting ready for. We have sometimes been fearful of turning students loose upon children for fear they might do them some very great damage. Every person who has ever been a child himself has had some experience with children and this ought to be capitalized upon at the earliest possible moment. Certainly it is true that we need to be responsible in the kinds of assignments we make. On the other hand, modern psychologists assure us that children are far tougher than we have been accustomed

[4] S. B. Sarason, K. Davidson, and B. Blott, *The Preparation of Teachers* (New York: Wiley, 1962).

to think. It takes a lot to destroy a child, and a single mistake, unless it is a matter of life and death, is not likely to be permanently damaging.

Personal Involvement With the Profession. Students entering the teaching profession ought to be encouraged to have as many contacts with teachers as possible. They ought to be seeing teachers on the job and off the job to the fullest extent the teachers can stand. They need to know teachers as people, to understand their problems, even to participate in their doubts and confusions. Young professional people ought also to be involved in every aspect of professional affairs. They need to be exposed to the great unsolved questions of the profession, to participate in debates upon salaries, grouping, merit pay, desegregation, or whatever the local and pressing problems of the profession are. They need to identify themselves early with the profession, so that these become "my" problems, rather than "their" problems.

Involvement With Fellow Students. Finally, the professional program must give its attention to helping students feel an important and integral part of the student body. We need to involve them intimately with each other, not only in the classroom but outside as well. In the basement of our college building is a cafeteria and coffee shop. The Florida Room, as it is known, is regarded by many of us on the faculty as the most important room in the building. It is probable that more real learning takes place in this student hangout than in most of the classrooms upstairs. The students get no grades for this activity. They are not even evaluated—but the faculty is!

THE CONDITIONS FOR EFFECTIVE LEARNING

To bring about the kind of learning we have been advocating for teacher education requires professional programs consciously and carefully designed to meet the three basic conditions for personal learning. These are

    1. The creation of student needs for understanding;
    2. The development of an atmosphere which makes the exploration of personal meaning possible; and

3.   Assistance and encouragement in the active exploration and discovery of personal meaning.

CREATING NEEDS FOR UNDERSTANDING

People do what they need to.   This is a basic principle of behavior all of us have known for a long time.   Yet, though we have known about it, we have not always effectively put it to work in teacher education.   Sometimes we have not utilized it because, like many of our students, we know about it but have not yet discovered its personal meaning for us.   Even when we have been aware of its importance, however, we may have failed to use it effectively for at least two reasons.

1.   We have failed to see things from the learner's point of view. While it is true that people always do what they need to—it is not true that they do what some outsider feels they need to do.   This difference in the perception of need has been a problem for generations.   Teachers are intent upon what young people will need to know twenty years from now, while students are interested in finding out what they need to know right now.

Teachers and students live in quite different worlds.   So it happens that the very knowledge possessed by the teacher may prevent him from perceiving the needs of his students.   It is a difficult thing for the expert, having achieved a particular level of knowledge or experience, to set all this aside and see things like a beginner.

2.   A second difficulty in relating teacher education to need has to do with the goals we have in mind.   Teacher-educators are often concerned with long-term goals, while the student is fundamentally motivated by short-term ones.   Looking at what a student will need to know six months, a year, two years from now, we operate on the assumption that he, too, perceives such goals as meaningful.   This seems logical enough but unfortunately it doesn't work out in practice. The needs which have a maximum degree of effect upon behavior are those needs the student perceives from moment to moment.   Though his professor may be quite certain that an understanding of Dewey's philosophy will be helpful to the student as a teacher, the relationship between Dewey's philosophy and his immediate needs is by no means so clearly apparent.   Since it is immediate needs which most strongly affect learning, we must create and utilize current needs in our students.

Teacher education must do much more than understand and satisfy student needs, however. A training program based solely on the satisfaction of student needs would not get very far. The genius of good teaching is not simply in the satisfaction of needs but in harnessing these needs to encourage a search for new goals and objectives which the student has never had before.

One of the least effective ways we can create needs is to tell students what is necessary to make them effective teachers. We have already seen that an emphasis on how teachers ought to behave is of limited help because it deals with symptoms, not with causes. The student who tries to behave in ways he does not understand or in ways unrelated to himself will find himself really frustrated.

The attempt to motivate teachers-in-training by discussions in perceptual terms of what makes a teacher is only a little more rewarding, because the previous experience of most students gets in the way of making this very effective. Most students have been so indoctrinated with the direct approach to behavioral change that the idea of seeking change through modification in their own beliefs and understandings often seems too complex and devious. It is hard to convince them that the time spent in looking, examining, exposing one's beliefs and ways of perceiving is not wasted. Because of their past experience many feel they are not learning anything unless they are being told more facts.

The most powerful needs, perceptual psychology tells us, are those which are seen as directly bearing upon the self. Anyone who has ever had the experience of teaching beginning teachers on a college campus concurrently with experienced teachers in the field can attest to the importance of having real problems to find answers to. Questions which seem to be of vital concern to teachers in the field may seem to the teacher-in-training on the campus as just another academic discussion. It is hard to get excited about artificial problems, but real ones, especially if they are one's own, have tremendous motivating power. This is not true of teaching alone. The importance of involvement in the training of professional workers is widely recognized in the other helping professions such as medicine, social work, nursing, psychology, and counseling.

Teacher educators have long been convinced of the importance of involvement. This is, in part, the function of practice teaching or the internship. Such involvement, however, is usually conceived as an opportunity to try what has already been learned, not as a means of creating the need to know.   As we are using the term here, we do not mean a period of involvement at the end of the student's program but an involvement at every step of the way from the very beginning of his entrance into the program.

DEVELOPING AN ATMOSPHERE FOR LEARNING

Learning is a function of the individual's personal exploration and discovery of meaning.   How likely this learning is to affect behavior of the individual will depend upon how important or close the idea is perceived in relation to the self.   The exploration of self does not occur, however, where circumstances are threatening or where the self is regarded as intruder.   Whether or not the exploration of self can occur will depend upon the atmospheres we create.

When people feel threatened, two interesting things happen to their abilities to perceive.   One of these is an effect which psychologists call "tunnel vision."   The field of perception becomes narrowed down so that they perceive only the object which threatens them. This experience is familiar to all of us.   We need but recall some instance when we have been seriously threatened to discover for ourselves how oblivious we became to the surrounding events in the midst of a threatening condition.   "I couldn't think of a thing!" we say, or, "All I could see was that——!"

A second effect of threat is to make the individual defend his existing position.   All of us are familiar with this dynamic too.   Generally, the more threatened the individual becomes, the more steadfastly he defends his existing position.   Now, clearly, these two effects of threat are antithetical to everything we are seeking in education. Surely we do not want students' perceptions to be narrowed.   On the contrary, we want them to be opened up.   Nor do we want individuals to defend their existing positions; we want them to change their positions to something more effective.   Since the individual's self is the most important and precious thing he owns, he is certainly not going to risk it in threatening situations.   It follows, then, that in order to help an individual explore and discover a more effective self, we must begin by creating atmospheres sufficiently free of threat so that the self can be explored and examined.   Like a turtle, the self cannot go anywhere unless it sticks its neck out.   But also like the turtle, the self will not venture forth from its shell unless it is safe enough out there to do so.

The elimination of threat from the learning situation does not mean that professors must coddle or shield prospective teachers. Quite the contrary, the task of teaching is to encourage and challenge students, to help them stretch themselves to their utmost. There is a difference between challenge and threat, however. Whether or not an individual feels challenged depends upon whether he feels he is able to deal with the situation with which he is confronted. If he feels he is not able to deal with the situation before him, the feeling he has is one of threat rather than challenge and the negative effects of threat we have described above are the consequence. The settings we need for the maximum professional growth are circumstances which challenge students but do not threaten them. To create this kind of atmosphere means that college instructors must be sensitive to the impact they have upon teachers-in-training, for the distinction between threat and challenge lies not in what the teacher thinks he is doing, but in what the students perceive him to be doing.

Basically, the atmosphere required for effective self-exploration is the same as that needed for the production of creativity, the expression of individuality. What restricts the individual's freedom to be and to express his deeper self makes him just that much less likely to be creative. Creativity is not learned from restraint. It calls for an atmosphere which encourages daring and venturing forth. Whatever narrows or hampers the exploration of ideas and the discovery of self must be rigorously eliminated from the teacher-education process. We need, rather, to find the very best means possible to create the kind of atmospheres which provide maximum freedom and openness of personality.

Two chapters of the 1962 ASCD Yearbook are devoted to a discussion of the ways in which teachers can encourage acceptance and openness to experience in children.[5] The suggestions are equally appropriate for adults hoping to be teachers themselves one day. The committee points out that conformity and creativity are antithetical— what produces one tends to destroy the other. The choice is clear. If we have conforming classrooms, we can be sure they will not be

[5] A. W. Combs, ed., *Perceiving, Behaving, Becoming: A New Focus for Education*, 1962 ASCD Yearbook (Washington, D. C.: Association for Supervision and Curriculum Development, 1962).

creative. If we want creative classrooms, we shall have to dispense with rigid controls, neatness, and externally imposed concepts of order. The atmosphere for self-discovery is one which calls for teachers who are friendly representatives of society, there to assist the growing process by eliminating what hinders self-discovery while encouraging and aiding what makes discovery possible. The following are a few of the factors listed by the Yearbook committee as hindrances to creativity and the atmosphere for growth:

1. Preoccupation with order, categorization, and classifying;
2. Overvaluing authority, support, evidence, and the "scientific method"—all the good answers are someone else's;
3. Exclusive emphasis upon the historical view, implying that all the good things have been discovered already;
4. Cookbook approaches, filling in the blanks, etc.;
5. Solitary learning, with its discouragement of communication;
6. The elimination of self from the classroom—only what the book says is important, not what I think;
7. Emphasis upon force, threat, or coercion. What diminishes the self diminishes creativity;
8. The idea that mistakes are sinful;
9. The idea that students are not to be trusted;
10. Lock-step organization.

On the other hand, the committee has suggested some of the following as factors producing atmospheres that encourage creativity:

1. The encouragement of fantasy and fun;
2. The provision of wide choices;
3. Trust in students so that they, in turn, can trust themselves;
4. Encouraging cooperative interaction;
5. Creating feelings of belonging;
6. Encouraging cooperation and discouraging competition;
7. Encouraging difference, uniqueness, and integrity;
8. Encouraging communication;
9. Encouraging problem-solving approaches;
10. Valuing openness and flexibility;
11. Valuing individuality;
12. Eliminating censorship;
13. Encouraging experimenting and trying.

Perhaps what is needed is the systematic examination of our teacher-education practices with an eye to the question of what encourages self-discovery.

ASSISTING THE DISCOVERY OF PERSONAL MEANING

Perceptual psychology has defined the basic principle of learning as the discovery of personal meaning. Whatever we hope will affect the behavior of the teacher-in-training must therefore be related to the student's self in important ways.

This important role of the self in teacher training may not be welcomed by some educators. For several generations we have treated scientific method and objectivity as sacred cows. For many, this has called for the rigorous exclusion of the self from learning and from the classroom situation. The emphasis has often been exclusively on facts, information, and the weight of evidence. If, however, the concept of learning advanced by modern perceptual psychology is accurate, the subjective experience of the individual must be admitted to the classroom.

In the old European universities the exploration and discovery of personal meaning was often accomplished in the interaction of students in the beer halls, which in those days were considered to be as vital a part of the university as the lecture hall. In this congenial setting students could get together to kick ideas around to their heart's content. In comparison, many aspects of the modern American university seem almost perversely designed to prevent the kind of personal involvement required for effective learning. Huge classes, the discouragement of student cooperation, content orientation, objective testing, and the ever-lengthening infancy we impose upon our young people de-emphasize the personal character of learning and discourage involvement of students in the learning process. The growth of interest in recent years in the utilization of discussion-group techniques seems at least one step in the right direction. We need many more.

This much seems certain—the personal exploration and discovery of meaning is not likely to occur unless it is valued by the faculty. To produce the kind of personal discovery of meaning about which we have been speaking, it will be necessary to place far less insistence upon the weight of authority, proof, and evidence while we encourage students to do their own looking, discovering, and thinking about professional problems. We will also need to encourage experimentation everywhere in the teacher-education program. This will not be easy, for one of the characteristics of our profession is that it has been built on "right answers." Facts, correctness, authority, proof, "100 per cent"—these have been the coin of the realm. To be wrong, to blunder, or to fail—these are things we have feared. Clearly, we cannot encourage experimentation and the personal discovery of meaning if making mistakes is practically synonymous with sinning. People learn from making mistakes, often more than from their successes. If we cannot permit mistakes, it should not surprise us if the product we turn out disappoints us with its conservatism and lack of imagination. People who are afraid to make mistakes will be afraid to try. People who do not try will surely not be creators or innovators. Somehow we must reverse this trend. Perhaps we need even to encourage students to make mistakes if this will foster experiment and exploration.

The personal discovery of meaning calls for a program in which differences are valued and encouraged, where wide choices are available, and where personal decisions are met with respect and admiration. Prejudice and censorship can have no part in such a program. There must be freedom to look at and try almost anything. To produce this kind of situation will require the careful analysis of programs for the elimination of barriers that lie in the path of student exploration and the active encouragement of difference and choice. Classrooms need to be seen as laboratories for trying, erring, reworking, and trying again.

4

The Good Teacher
Is Well Informed

THE FIRST OF THE FIVE CHARACTERISTICS attributed to the effective teacher in Chapter 2 was "a rich, extensive, and available field of perceptions about his subject." In other words, a good teacher must be well informed. This seems so obvious as to need no statement at all. Many critics of modern education, however, do not feel so.[1] Hearing teacher educators talking much about the adjustment of the child, the process of learning, the philosophy and history of education, and so on, they become honestly concerned over what seems to them a de-emphasis of solid intellectual accomplishment in favor of such matters. The critics need have no fear, however. Professional educators are keenly aware that teachers need to be well informed.

What seems like a lack of concern to the critic is actually an artifact of the way in which most teacher education in the United States is organized. Many teacher-education programs, particularly those in large universities, have little, if any, control over the subject-matter preparation of their students. This portion of teacher education is the responsibility of the traditional academic departments in the university. Typically, the student teachers' experience with subject matter is acquired from these scholars while the professional educator is assigned the responsibility for the how and why of teaching. What seems like a lack of concern for subject matter is often a mere product of the division of labor. People naturally talk most about the things they are responsible for.

The purpose of this book is to explore the professional aspects of teacher education. The content preparation of teachers is a subject

[1] J. D. Koerner, *The Miseducation of American Teachers* (Boston: Houghton Mifflin, 1963).

for several other books. However, the successful professional school cannot ignore the student's subject-matter experiences even if it has no direct control over them. The student's experience with his teachers in the content areas provides him with a live demonstration of his subject being taught. The subject-matter professor is teaching the *way to teach* as well as *what to teach,* even though this may not be his intention at all. What students learn as a consequence of this experience is often much more lasting than that which they are only told about. There is a saying among teacher educators that "students teach like they have been taught rather than the way we taught them to teach." Students do not enter the teacher-preparation program without experience in teaching. They enter with twelve or fifteen years of having been taught.

Professional education must spend much time helping students see that there are other ways of teaching than those they may have been exposed to thus far. Often this is not easy. It is difficult for students to learn to discount their past experiences. Nor is it easy to persuade professors to change their ways of teaching. There is nothing more sacrosanct on a college campus than academic freedom, which often may be interpreted to mean the professor's inalienable right to teach excruciatingly badly! The subject-matter preparation of teachers cannot be ignored, however, and the educator must continually use his influence to improve the quality of subject-matter teaching wherever and whenever possible. In the remainder of this chapter let us examine some of the more outstanding factors which seem related to the subject-matter preparation of teachers.

THE SELECTION OF CONTENT

SOME FACTORS IN CONTENT SELECTION

Teachers need to be well informed. But about what? Once it was easy to answer that question, but the answers are no longer so simple. Three current factors that make it difficult to determine what teachers need to know are the information explosion, changing social needs, and changing concepts of what information is pertinent.

The Information Explosion. The amount of information available to human beings today is so much greater than that possessed by our forebears as to stagger the imagination. There was a time when comparatively few subjects, once mastered, could guarantee that a man might live for the rest of his days revered as a scholar and a wise man by his fellows. But those days are gone forever! The facts known to man have proliferated at such speed that a scholar today can count himself lucky if he is able to encompass in a lifetime all that is known even in a very limited field of knowledge.

When I was in teachers college in 1934, I remember solemnly writing down in one of my education classes this objective of education: "The goal of education is passing on to the new generation the accumulated culture of man's experience." I do not recall that anyone laughed at such a statement. It seemed eminently right and attainable in those days. But who would be so brash today as to suggest that education could really hope to achieve so vast a goal?

To be well informed in these times is a quite different thing than it was fifty, or even twenty, years ago. The old concepts of what is essential are no longer valid. There is no longer a set body of information to be required of everyone, only a vast body of facts from which to make choices.

The Changing Needs of Society. The proper selection of content for teachers is further complicated by the increasing variety of human needs. Adam Smith wrote in 1776, that man's needs were for food, shelter, and clothing. Even in those days, however, such a definition of human need was only partly true. In the replete societies of today, it is totally inadequate. The extent of modern man's needs seems almost limitless. The schooling needed for the wealthy dilettante of generations ago is a far cry from the needs of the modern citizen with a job to do and responsibilities to meet in a more and more complicated world. When choices were limited, we could be quite sure about what was good to know. With the choices open to us today who shall say with certainty what any man *must* know?

This much is certain: The narrow curriculum suitable a hundred years ago is as out of date now as the horse and buggy. We expect our schools to provide us with a vast army of persons able to assume the duties and carry out the functions of a tremendously complex technological existence. No single curriculum can provide us with such diversity. A variety of teachers with many different skills are called for.

Changing Concepts of Teacher Needs for Information. What the teacher needs to know will depend upon his particular professional task. The good teacher needs all the information he can get, but not all information is of equal importance for him. What information is required will depend upon the level he is expected to teach, the nature and backgrounds of his students, the equipment available, the needs of students and community, and a hundred other factors. The kind and depth of content required for the primary, elementary, junior high, senior high, and junior college teacher varies greatly depending upon the particular responsibilities the well-informed teacher must carry out.[2]

It is apparent that the concept of the teacher as wise man and fountainhead of information is long outmoded. Once we could expect that most of the facts required by his students would be at the teacher's fingertips. But where could one find such a teacher today? A kindergarten teacher, accustomed to thinking of herself as fairly well informed, recently reported with some shock the amused toleration of her class as they set her straight on space terminology! Today's teacher will often be working with students far better informed than he in dozens of areas, sometimes, in the very area the teacher is trying to teach!

Even if we could hope to produce a teacher with the "right" information for today's world it would almost certainly not be right for tomorrow's. Education is one of the few industries to turn out its product twenty years *after* the demand. Since we cannot foresee the future with certainty, we cannot hope to teach today all that people must know tomorrow. Our only salvation is the production of intelligent people. For that we need intelligent teachers, *knowing* persons. This "knowing" may be quite general or highly specific. Either way, teacher education must produce intelligent, informed human beings. Mere storehouses of information are not enough.

It is always a temptation in looking for answers to educational problems to seek across-the-board solutions that can be applied in all times and in all places. This usually turns out to be a pipe dream. Such solutions simply do not exist. The same content demands cannot be made of all students in training for the profession. We cannot

[2] G. W. Denemark, ed., *Criteria for Curriculum Decisions in Teacher Education* (Washington, D. C.: Association for Supervision and Curriculum Development, 1964).

expect a kindergarten or first-grade teacher to have the specialized knowledge of the instructor in astronomy at the college level. Nor can we demand of the high-school teacher that he have at his instant command the ingenious array of information and techniques required of the busy kindergarten teacher. What is needed is both a broad general education designed for the development of intelligent, effective citizens and a program of specialization aimed at preparing the teacher for the particular professional task he will later be expected to fill.

THE GENERAL EDUCATION PROGRAM

The making of a teacher begins with an intelligent layman. For the preparation of teachers we need the best general education program we are able to devise.[3] Such a program does not need to be specially devised for teachers. Neither should it be a watered-down affair taught with disdain for people who are not going to major in the subject. Teachers need the same high quality program in general education that we seek for all beginning college students. Indeed, because they are going to be teachers, this is more important for them than for anyone.

Unhappily the level of teaching in general education programs in many of our colleges leaves much to be desired. Overwhelmed with students and charged with the responsibility for "weeding them out," harassed instructors often cover the subject as best they can and escape as quickly as possible to teaching the majors. As a consequence, general education programs are often badly taught and deadly dull. This is not good for any student. For education students it is disastrous.

CONTENT SPECIALIZATION

In addition to his general education preparation, the student teacher needs one or more areas of specialization in the particular content which he will be responsible for teaching. This is usually acquired by selecting courses from those offered by the various subject-matter departments of the college or university. The provision of these courses has always been the prime function of colleges. Many provide

---

[3] Margaret Lindsey, *New Horizons for the Teaching Profession* (Washington, D. C.: National Commission on Teacher Education and Professional Standards, N. E. A., 1961).

very rich and rewarding opportunities for learning. For students expecting to teach specific subjects in high school or junior college, this kind of course organization presents no great problem. For the student planning to teach in an area cutting across subject-matter lines, however, or for the teacher preparing to work in the elementary grades, it is another matter. Their subject-matter needs often do not fit the traditional college pattern.[4]

The elementary teacher has a specialty. It is teaching general education. For this he needs preparation in breadth over a number of subjects rather than depth in one or two, but few colleges are organized to provide this for him. Courses in the various subject-matter departments are generally designed with majors in mind and tend to become increasingly specialized, so that the student who should spread his attention over a number of areas can seldom acquire the kind of experience he needs.

In some colleges the failure to understand the task of the elementary teacher has created morale problems as well. It has sometimes happened, for example, that elementary teachers have been accused of ignorance and treated as second-class citizens by professors who have equated depth of knowledge with scholarship. This is most unfair. The elementary teacher's specialization in general education is legitimate and necessary. It is a different order of specialization but surely not a less important one! The content required for general education is not less, only broader.

THE TEACHING OF CONTENT

In the light of our new understandings concerning the learner and the learning process, what can we perceive about the teaching of content? Here are some guidelines that grow out of our new concepts.

MAKING CONTENT MEANINGFUL

Content must be meaningful; it is not an end in itself. It is not enough to produce teachers who *collect* facts. We must find ways of producing teachers who *find meaning in* facts and who help their students to do so. There are limits to what any teacher can or should

---

[4] G. K. Hodenfield and T. M. Stinnett, *The Education of Teachers* (Englewood Cliffs, N. J.: Prentice-Hall, 1961).

know. Whether we like it or not, we shall often have to be content with having our children taught by teachers who do not know all about the subject. The good teacher's task is to stimulate and facilitate learning. The measure of his success is not the degree to which his students are like him, but the degree to which he has assisted his students to transcend him.

Facts are no more than tools for the solution of problems. There are no facts which a person must know except in the light of his purposes and goals. As Johnson and Swan have expressed it,

> The simple addition of more and more facts does not produce better and better education. If this were true, teaching children would be a pretty simple and straightforward proposition. We could simply add more of everything: more time in the school years, more hours in the school day, more pages in books, more facts for the memory. It is possible though that we have already reached the saturation level from the standpoint of "more" and we may be justified in viewing with alarm the degree to which we sacrifice reasoning and thinking on the altar of content. Perhaps it is equally true that we substitute presenting facts to our students for presenting seasoned and matured thinking of our own. The simple recitation of facts and the demanding of their recall on schedule is an effective way to dodge the issue of thinking for ourselves and for suggesting challenging ideas. It is disquieting to consider this: if our recital of facts were stripped from us would we stand intellectually naked in front of the class?[5]

It is only as the meaning of facts is perceived that they become useful and effective tools for the advancement of human understanding and happiness. It is this concern for meaning which has caused many teachers to be increasingly concerned with the *structure* of content rather than the collection and dissemination of facts. Bruner has expressed the matter in this way:

> Mastery of the fundamental ideas of a field involves not only the grasping of general principles, but also the development of an attitude toward learning and inquiry, toward guessing and hunches, toward the possibility of solving problems on one's own. Just as a physicist has certain attitudes about the ultimate orderliness of nature and a conviction that order can be discovered, so a young physics student needs some working version of these attitudes if he is to organize his learning in such a way as to make what he learns useable and meaningful in his thinking. To instill such attitudes by teaching requires something more than the mere presentation of fundamental ideas. Just what it takes to bring off such

---

[5] V. B. Johnson and Beverly Swan, "Cult of Content," *Ed. Leadership,* 1961, **19,** 118–121.

teaching is something on which a great deal of research is needed, but it would seem that an important ingredient is a sense of excitement about discovery—discovery of regularities of previously unrecognized relations and similarities between ideas, with a resulting sense of self-confidence in one's abilities.[6]

The current concern for the structure of content seems like an important step forward. Its value, however, may be subverted if it is seen as no more than an emphasis upon principles rather than details in the teaching of content. Meaning is not a function of the organization of subject matter. It is not something given to the student, but something the student discovers for himself. He does not acquire it from outside, he finds it within himself. The discovery of meaning is a personal process involving the student's own purposes, values, goals, concepts, and needs. The organization of content and the emphases of the instructor can help in the process of discovering meaning. It is no guarantee that the discovery will occur.

Unhappily the discovery of meaning by students is often badly impeded in many college classrooms by an emphasis on trifling detail. Concepts and generalizations in any subject are comparatively few, but details are myriad. An instructor talking about generalizations would quickly run out of material, but he can talk about details forever! Small wonder that students "get the message" that "the instructor believes details are the important things."

Detail by itself is meaningless. Unless detail is placed in an overall pattern it is rapidly forgotten. One needs but to watch a group of college students preparing for their examinations to understand how thoroughly they have been impressed with the importance of detail. They know that good grades depend not upon one's grasp of generalizations, but upon one's ability to demonstrate knowledge of details. To make matters worse, we are committed to a grading system which requires the distribution of students along a continuum. The more they can be spread out, the easier it is to assign and justify grades. But with better and better students coming to college as a consequence of tighter patterns of selection the only way in which such a spread can be produced is through testing students more and more intensively on the nonessentials. So we are forced by the demands of

[6] J. S. Bruner, *The Process of Education* (New York: Vintage Books, 1963).

our examination and grading system to be preoccupied with details at the expense of meaning. It is a responsibility of the teacher-education curriculum to combat this creeping paralysis whenever it occurs, both inside and outside its immediate area of responsibility. What good is a teacher who knows facts but not what they mean?

In the past twenty years we have come to see the process of learning as an emerging process. We now understand it as a matter of exploring and discovering on the part of the student rather than a process of injection on the part of the teacher. This shift in our thinking has paid vast dividends everywhere in public education. This does not mean that an organized, systematic consideration of subject matter is per se antithetical to student-centered teaching. It is quite possible for a teacher to be deeply student-centered in his approach to teaching while at the same time his work is organized around a systematized body of subject matter. The problem is not to be stated as either/or; it is rather, What is the place of organized approaches to subject matter in student-centered learning? Since the codification and organization of principles can only follow the acquisition of facts and principles, the beginner in any discipline must be much less concerned with the organization of knowledge than he will be at later stages in his development. As Bode expressed it, the student must begin with a *psychological order* of subject matter and end with a *logical order*. At later stages of a given topic the student himself will need his subject matter to be system-oriented. The teacher who provides an organized body of subject matter for the consideration of such a student is also operating within the concept of student-oriented teaching.

RELATING CONTENT TO STUDENT PURPOSES

Instructors who work with education students must be aware that the purposes of such students may be quite different from liberal arts students in the very same classes. It is a basic principle of learning that whatever is learned is a function of the purposes of the learner. It follows, therefore, that whatever is taught in subject-matter classes needs to be closely related to the purposes of the students. In their enthusiasm for their subject, professors often find it hard to believe that others do not find their topic as fascinating and exciting as they do themselves. Subject matter is, therefore, often taught as though all students were committed to devoting their lives to the study of that subject. Some of them may. But the person preparing to teach usually has no intention of doing deep research in the subject. If he is a grade-school teacher, he may even be interested in the subject only as it contributes to his general background. Even students who are preparing to teach at the secondary level may have chosen the teaching profession because they are interested in working with young people and so regard subject matter as the *vehicle* they use to teach rather than something to be learned for its own sake.

Teachers are practitioners. Their concern is with the dissemination, application, and use of information. It is to be hoped they might be scholars too, but not in the same sense as one would expect of the student preparing to spend his life in research. This view of the uses of subject matter often lands the education student right in the middle of the practitioner-scholar controversy we discussed at the beginning of Chapter 3. In all innocence he may find himself sitting in classes surrounded by students who see themselves as scholars, experts, and scientists and who hold education students in contempt. He may even be so unlucky as to find that the professor himself subscribes to such attitudes. Although the neophyte teacher's purposes are different, they are not unimportant. We cannot afford to produce teachers who see themselves as second-rate and who must apologize for being what they are. Nor can we afford to produce teachers whose own experience with subject matter has brought them to the conclusion that the way to get subject matter across is through the humiliation and embarrassment of students.

COMMUNICATING EFFECTIVELY

The student's grasp of content will be determined in large measure by the success of the instructor in communicating it. Communication, regarded by some instructors as an automatic concomitant of presenting the subject matter, is much more than this; it is a skill to be learned in its own right, and it has not occurred until something happens in the learner.

It is a common complaint of professors that students do not hear or understand what they are trying to tell them. The usual assumption is that the student is not meeting his responsibility. For example, I recently heard a college professor complain that it was *necessary to fail over 50 per cent of his class.* To him this was a clear indication that modern students are stupid and/or lazy. This in spite of the fact that college students today are more highly selected than ever before in history! The question might well be raised, Who has failed—the student or the teacher?

The primary responsibility for communication is always with the communicator, not the listener, and the teacher need not sacrifice scholarship to be understood. Einstein enjoyed talking to adolescents, and many of our most famous scientists have been able to communicate effectively with Congressional committees.

Another factor interfering with effective communication is the widespread belief that students should be introduced to subject matter cafeteria-style, in which all possible points of view are presented. It seems logical that the way to produce an open-minded, well-informed scholar is to confront him with all the possible data and let him arrive at his own best conclusions. Unfortunately, people do not learn logically. Learning is a question of meaning, and meaning is a matter of discovering the interrelationships of things. Discovery may actually be impeded by too great a flood of data. There is a world of difference between the situation experienced by the learned scholar critically looking at many points of view from the security of his established position and that of the beginner asked to cope with a bewildering flood of ideas without such security. Knowing a subject and knowing about it are by no means the same. Communication is not just a matter of presenting data. It is a function of discovery and development of meanings.

INVOLVING THE STUDENT IN THE SUBJECT MATTER

No matter how well subject matter is presented, it will have no effect upon the student until he has become personally involved in the learning process. Learning is not passive. It is an active process, requiring a personal commitment on the part of the learner. A great deal of college teaching violates this principle.

The impersonality of much of our teaching was bad enough in years past. With television and teaching machines we now seek to teach students by the hundreds without the teacher present at all! There is no doubt that a kind of rote learning, sufficient to pass examinations, can often be experienced by students under these circumstances. It is not enough for prospective teachers. The student who

People do not learn logically. Learning is a question of meaning, & meaning is a matter of discovering the interrelationships of things.

is going out to teach must have a much deeper, more meaningful grasp of content than this.

The terrible competition for grades which has become a normal part of college curricula has a negative effect on developing student commitment. Grades limit and inhibit learning. The kind of knowing required for getting A's seldom leaves room for the student's own purposes or involvement. It is guessing what the instructor thinks is important and parroting it back to him with efficiency that pays off. Students quickly learn to set aside their own interests and to spend their energies in memorization rather than understanding.

Many of our most hallowed college traditions seem expressly designed to prevent the kind of involvement we now know is essential to effective learning. So much effort is expended in teaching the student what is already known that little time or opportunity remains to enable him to discover what he can for himself. The scholar certainly needs to know and respect the work of his forebears but this can be carried too far. The student who learns that all the good answers, all the right answers, all the approved answers lie "out there" in what others have done or said or thought may end by becoming apathetic or discouraged at the possibilities of his own contributions. In a world needing creative people as much as ours, this is a wasteful, even dangerous, occurrence. In order to become effective teachers, teachers-in-training need to *experience* subject matter, to wade around in it, to make mistakes in it, to be intensely and personally in interaction with it, till it becomes a part of their very being. They must feel they are participants in it and contributors to it.

THE NEED FOR INSPIRED INSTRUCTION

It is essential that young people setting out to become teachers experience a sense of the wonder as well as the toil of learning a subject. To acquire this they need contact with the most inspiring and enthusiastic instructors available in the subject-matter areas. But often such instructors are available only in specialized courses taken by subject-matter majors, or their time is much occupied with research or administrative duties. This is a great pity. All our students, particularly those preparing for the teaching profession, need as much inspired instruction as they can get.

We cannot afford to turn out dull and pedantic teachers, for these discourage students and subvert the purposes of education. The genius of good teaching lies in the capacity to fire the imagination. It is the satisfaction of search and discovery that motivates learning and provides new knowledge. If we are to produce teachers capable of such inspired teaching, we must select the most inspired teachers for them. It is a curious thing that our deep reverence for the scientific method often expresses itself in the dullest of teaching. Many instructors try so hard to be "detached" that they end up "out of touch." But to care about one's subject is not unscientific, and the rigor and respect for his subject demanded of the scientist are not incompatible with excitement and enthusiasm.

UNDERSTANDING THE NATURE OF LEARNING

Since teacher-education students learn from their own experience not only subject matter but also how to teach it, teacher-preparation programs cannot afford to overlook this aspect of teacher training. They must be concerned about the quality of subject-matter teaching wherever their students learn it and must do much more to disseminate what is known about the process of learning among their confreres elsewhere in the college or university. There is a gulf between the best we know about learning and its implementation in practice. It is imperative that this lag between knowledge and practice be reduced as quickly as possible—not only for teacher-education students but for all college students. Ways must be found to introduce into the thinking of teachers at every level the very best concepts of the nature of learning that we have.

Wider understanding of the learning process might go far toward reducing some of the most destructive criticism currently leveled at teachers and the programs they come from. Many of the things teachers do are attempts to put into operation modern concepts about the process of learning. To persons outside education who conceive of learning as a simple process of telling and listening, these things may seem quite unrelated to the job to be done.

It is often assumed that learning is a simple process of presentation and absorption. Learning is rarely seen as a process to be investigated by scientific methods. Like many other human interrelationships it is lived with, dealt with daily, but seldom regarded as a matter to be studied or subjected to the scientific procedures that have carried us so far in other spheres of life. Learning *is* subject to scrutiny and there *are* things we know about it. Teacher-education curricula are based upon the assumption that learning is a lawful, predictable, teachable function. This is their reason for being.

The knowledge we have about learning has been acquired in the same painstaking, carefully controlled kind of experimentation which has made possible the great advances of the other sciences. It is composed of facts and principles about an important human process and it deserves the same respect and understanding as any other body of scientific knowledge. Once it was my privilege to work as a consultant with the faculty of a college of agriculture who were interested in improving the teaching methods used in their college. I spoke to them of the things we know that affect the efficiency of learning. Among these were such things as the relationship of learning to student motivation, needs, readiness, perception, meaning, and emotional condition on the one hand, and the atmosphere and conditions of learning on the other, including such matters as the role of the teacher, the principles of effective communication, the effects of threat and coercion, and the utilization of various sense modalities in learning. During the discussion which followed a professor of agronomy complained about this complexity. "Mr. Combs," he said, "all this may be very well for you as an educational psychologist, but it has nothing to do with the teaching of agronomy. I do not have time to be concerned about such things. I have all I can do just to get my subject across"! This same professor, because of his careful study of soils, knows that in order to grow a plant well it is necessary to deal with all the conditions affecting growth—amount of moisture, proper balance of acidity and alkalinity, and so on. He would not think of telling the farmer to forget these conditions any more than he would say, "I know my car needs a carburetor to run, but I'm going to run mine without one!" Yet in his own teaching he does exactly that. The principles of learning can no more be suspended than any other scientifically derived understanding. They continue to operate whether we are aware of them or not. If we ignore them, we do so at the risk of making our teaching haphazard and ineffective.

PREPARATION AS A NEVER-ENDING PROCESS

Many young people entering teaching seem to have the notion that preparation for teaching a subject is completed upon graduation from college. They have an idea that Shakespeare, algebra, or dress design is a kind of unit, capable of completion, instead of an on-going, never-ending area for search and discovery. College courses may often be but a minor part of professional preparation. No course, or program of courses, can ever hope to provide the teacher with all the answers to all the problems he will confront in the course of his teaching experience. Nor should they try to.

In recent years we have had some beautiful examples of this misconception about subject matter brought home to us. We have awakened to discover that many of our teachers are woefully behind the current position of knowledge in their fields, especially in the fields of mathematics and science. New discovery moves at such a pace in almost every field of study that it does not take long to fall out of date even with the best of undergraduate preparation. Like *Alice In Wonderland* one must run as fast as one can just to stay where one is.

Effective preparation in subject matter is not just a question of the accumulation of credits. It is the development of an attitude of continual research and discovery. Teachers are not merely disseminators of subject matter, they are participants in it. The training of teachers in subject matter must instill in them a problem-solving approach to their subject and a need for never-ending preparation. Teacher-training curricula must exert every influence to see that students are exposed to such approaches to subject matter. Every effort must be exerted to improve the levels of teaching, not just from kindergarten through high school but also at the college level.

5

The Teacher's Beliefs About People

THE PROFESSIONAL TRAINING OF TEACHERS must begin with the student's beliefs about people. A prime requisite for good teaching is the clearest, most useful understanding of the nature of people and their behavior existing in our generation, because teachers, like everyone else, behave in terms of what seems to them to be so. A false or inaccurate conception of what his students are like provides the teacher with an inadequate basis for making decisions and directing the learning process. Only when the teacher's perceptions about student behavior are accurate and available when he needs them can we be sure his attempts to teach will be effective.

THE EFFECTIVE TEACHER'S CONCEPTS ABOUT PEOPLE

What kinds of beliefs about people are characteristic of effective professional workers? A series of researches at the University of Florida investigated the perceptual differences between good and poor professional workers in teaching,[1,2,3] counseling,[4] and the ministry.[5] From

[1] A. W. Combs, "The Personal Approach to Good Teaching," *Ed. Leadership*, 1964, **21**, 369–378.

[2] C. T. Gooding, "An Observational Analysis of the Perceptual Organization of Effective Teachers," Unpublished Ed.D. Dissertation (Gainesville: Univ. of Florida, 1964).

[3] Deleted.

[4] A. W. Combs and D. W. Soper, "Perceptual Organization of Effective Counselors," *J. Counsel. Psych.*, 1963, **10**, No. 3, 222–226.

[5] John A. Benton, "Perceptual Characteristics of Episcopal Pastors," Unpublished Ed.D. Dissertation (Gainesville: Univ. of Florida, 1964).

54

these studies, it appears that good teachers can be clearly distinguished from poor ones with respect to the following beliefs about people:

Internal-External Frame of Reference. The good teacher's general frame of reference can be described as internal rather than external; that is to say, he seems sensitive to and concerned with how things seem to others with whom he interacts and uses this as a basis for his own behavior.[6]

People-Things Orientation. Central to the thinking of the good teacher is a concern with people and their reactions rather than with things and events.[6,7]

Meanings-Facts Orientation. The good teacher is more concerned with the perceptual experience of people than with the objective events. He is sensitive to how things seem to people rather than being exclusively concerned with concrete events.[6]

Immediate-Historical Causation. The good teacher seeks the causes of people's behavior in their current thinking, feeling, beliefs, and understandings rather than in objective descriptions of the forces exerted upon them now or in the past.[6]

Able-Unable. The good teacher perceives others as having the capacities to deal with their problems. He believes that they can find adequate solutions to events, as opposed to doubting the capacity of people to handle themselves and their lives.[6]

Friendly-Unfriendly. The good teacher sees others as being friendly and enhancing. He does not regard them as threatening to himself but rather sees them as essentially well-intentioned rather than evil-intentioned.[6]

Worthy-Unworthy. The good teacher tends to see other people as being of worth rather than unworthy. He sees them as possessing a dignity and integrity which must be respected and maintained rather than seeing them as unimportant, as people whose integrity may be violated or treated as of little account.[6,7]

Internally-Externally Motivated. The good teacher sees people and their behavior as essentially developing from within rather than as a

---

[6] True of counselors also. Combs and Soper, *op. cit.*
[7] True of priests also. Benton, *op. cit.*

product of external events to be molded, directed; sees people as creative, dynamic rather than passive or inert.[6]

Dependable-Undependable. The good teacher sees people as essentially trustworthy and dependable in the sense of behaving in a lawful way. He regards their behavior as understandable rather than capricious, unpredictable, or negative.[6]

Helpful-Hindering. The good teacher sees people as being potentially fulfilling and enhancing to self rather than impeding or threatening. He regards people as important sources of satisfaction rather than sources of frustration and suspicion.

No doubt other research studies will add to this list in time. Meanwhile, the factors described in these studies provide us with guideposts to action. They describe some of the kinds of beliefs about people that students need to acquire in the course of training and suggest some factors in the kinds of programs we need in order to bring such perceptions into being.

HELPING STUDENTS FORMULATE ADEQUATE CONCEPTS ABOUT PEOPLE

Since perceptions are acquired from experience, there seem to be four avenues by which students may develop adequate beliefs about people: from the study of behavior; from personal experience of faculty beliefs and values; from the ways they are treated by the college staff; through personal involvement with children and adults.

THE CONTRIBUTION OF TRADITIONAL PSYCHOLOGY

The need for understanding about people and behavior is widely recognized and has long been a part of the curriculum. Almost every teacher-education curriculum includes such courses as Human Growth and Development, the Psychology of Childhood, the Psychology of Adolescence, Educational Psychology, or similar courses designed to acquaint the teacher-in-training with the best that is known about human behavior.

For the most part these approaches to understanding behavior have been based upon the stimulus-response concept characteristic of

American psychology for at least fifty years. This frame of reference seeks the causes of behavior in the forces at work upon the individual from his heredity, his physiological condition, or his environment. Its basic tenet is that the behavior of people is the product of the forces to which they have been subjected in the process of growing up. It is essentially a descriptive, diagnostic view of behavior.

This view of behavior marked a great step forward for the social sciences when it first appeared, and it has provided the basis for many of the important contributions in those disciplines. It has also had a tremendous influence throughout our society generally. Its concepts are on everyone's tongue, and its principles are applied more or less successfully everywhere. In education it has been valuable in providing a frame of reference for attacking many problems of the profession. For thousands of teachers, for example, it has provided a background against which the behavior of children could be more adequately understood. For administrators and supervisors it has provided essential data for curriculum revision and program planning.

Despite its contributions, however, stimulus-response psychology has three serious inadequacies which prevent it from making the larger contributions educators need: 1) It is essentially mechanistic rather than personalistic. That is to say, it provides us with important information about what *people in general* are like or what *people in general* may do but often leaves us in the dark with respect to understanding the particular person in a particular setting. 2) It is diagnostically rather than treatment oriented. It tells us, often very effectively, how people get like this or what forces caused a given behavior to occur but adds very little to helping us know what needs to be done about the matter. 3) It is often inconsistent with modern educational philosophy. Traditional psychology is essentially mechanistic and manipulative whereas modern educational philosophy calls for a growth or facilitating approach to teaching.

The traditional approach to psychology prides itself on being "hard-nosed," on studying people objectively, scientifically, and dispassionately. This has been fruitful in providing us with much important information about human behavior. But the kinds of beliefs about people described in the research mentioned above are not acquired from information alone. Knowledge of facts about behavior may contribute to the development of beliefs, but it cannot be counted upon to produce them single-handed.

THE CONTRIBUTIONS OF PERCEPTUAL PSYCHOLOGY

The inclusion of perceptual-existential approaches to psychology in teacher-training programs has provided many teachers with a second pair of glasses through which to look at behavior. Perceptual psychology is a personal, dynamic, treatment-oriented view of behavior invented very largely by clinical psychologists, whose problem, like that of the teacher, is the behavior of individuals. It is a psychology directly concerned with human perceptions, beliefs, and values, and many teacher-preparation programs have already incorporated this frame of reference into their curricula. It fits so well the needs of educators as to seem almost tailor-made for the teaching profession.

We have already pointed out in Chapter 2 how perceptual psychology emphasizes the personal qualities of human experience. It seeks the causes of behavior in meanings. It is also more directly action-oriented. Teachers need a psychology which makes it possible to deal with children in the present, in the here-and-now, face-to-face relationship of the classroom. It must offer clues about *people* who learn, as well as the *process* of learning. Perceptual psychology does this.

It assures the teacher that he can be a helpful force even in the life of the most difficult child. If behavior is a function of perception, then, if we can understand how the child is perceiving in the present, there are things we can do right now to help him grow and develop— even if we know nothing whatever about his past or his family life!

A point of view about human behavior which demands the manipulation and control of the individual's environment in order to help him has serious limitations for treatment. The older the child gets, the larger and larger the world to which he is responding becomes, and the less we have a chance of controlling and redirecting that world. It is a simple thing to remove candy from the neighborhood of a baby. The problems involved in removing alcohol from the path of the full-grown adult, however, are quite a different matter! The older the individual grows, the more we must depend upon producing a change in his personal world rather than in the outer world in which he happens to be moving. This calls for changes in how he is seeing and believing and feeling about things. It also calls for sensitivity and understanding in those who would help him. One must acquire the ability to feel and perceive as another does. The preparation of such empathic teachers requires a perceptual psychology.

The value of the perceptual view of behavior is by no means restricted to mental hygiene problems. Learning itself is a matter of perceiving. Unless a child perceives differently, he hasn't learned at all. It is the goal of education to produce citizens capable of perceiving more broadly, more accurately, and more richly. This calls for teachers who are keenly aware of the perceptual world of their students and who can as a result facilitate the processes of learning. Understanding arithmetic, literature, physical education, or geography is a question of perceiving, and the teacher equipped with a perceptual view of behavior will be more adequately prepared to help children grow intellectually as well as emotionally. Individual, perceptual, or personalistic psychology is consistent with the democratic belief that when men are free to explore and discover they can find their own best ways. It is also consistent with modern educational beliefs and practices.

To many teachers the perceptual view of behavior comes as a refreshing breeze. It means that what they do is always important. Teachers and children are not merely victims of circumstance; there are things they can do to control their destinies and guide their fates. It is a fascinating and heart-warming experience to watch the excitement of experienced teachers exposed to perceptual views of behavior for the first time. It speaks to them in language they understand and provides practical answers to knotty problems that have harried them for years. They find in it a new tool especially suited to their tasks. New teacher-education students pick up the perceptual view naturally and easily. It fits their experience so smoothly they think they have always known it!

The first three characteristics of good teachers reported in the research at the beginning of this chapter are all ways of looking at people in the very manner prescribed by perceptual psychology. Most of the teachers in these experiments had never heard of perceptual psychology, yet they had somehow learned to look at their students in this fashion. Apparently, good teachers arrive at this frame of reference with respect to people as a consequence of their experience. If this is true, it is time we introduced it much more widely to our teacher-training programs. Educators cannot afford to let their curricula fall out of date. The lag between the best that psychology can supply us and its introduction to teacher-education programs must be kept as small as possible. Third Force psychology is at least thirty years old now and what it has to offer teacher education is too important to ignore.

SOME SUGGESTIONS FOR CONTENT

Perceptual psychology does more than provide the educator with a view of man consistent with his philosophy and practice. It also offers a considerable body of content capable of helping teachers develop the kinds of beliefs about people characteristic of good teachers. Some of this content is derived from a perceptual interpretation of information about behavior which good teacher-education programs have included for many years. Some comes from the growing body of theory and research being developed by personalistic psychologists.

As we have previously pointed out, perceptual psychology does not deny other psychological thought. What we know of man from traditional viewpoints is still as true as it ever was. A new frame of reference does not wipe away what has gone before. It only reinterprets the past and extends itself to new problems not adequately dealt with before.

Looking at the psychological content for new teachers from a perceptual orientation causes us to reaffirm some traditional material we have always found helpful, to eliminate some traditional material in favor of more auspicious concepts for teaching, and to add a number of quite new areas of investigation which hold much promise for the production of effective teachers.

Recent research on the perceptual organization of teachers suggests that good teachers typically perceive students as able, friendly, worthy, dependable, and internally motivated.[8,9] Such beliefs about people may, of course, be acquired from one's own experience with them. The support of study, research, and psychological theory can make them more secure. Beliefs are more likely to serve as effective guides for behavior when they are consistent with the facts we have been able to acquire. This requires a consideration by young teachers of what is known about people from all points of view and the integration of this information into the student's own world of thinking and feeling. Extracting from the whole field of psychological thought

[8] Gooding, *op. cit.*
[9] Deleted.

those aspects most likely to be helpful to teachers, I have arrived at the list of topics indicated below. No doubt others would arrive at a quite different list. This one is mine, chosen deliberately from the perceptual frame of reference.

TOPICS CHOSEN FROM TRADITIONAL AND PERCEPTUAL PSYCHOLOGY MOST LIKELY TO BE HELPFUL IN THE PREPARATION OF NEW TEACHERS

1. The nature of perception and its relation to behavior
   a. How we gather information about behavior
   b. The development of sensitivity to people
2. The nature and function of human need
   a. The origin of purposes
   b. The refinement of purpose into goals and values
   c. The effects of need, goals, and values on behavior
3. The self-concept
   a. What it is
   b. How it develops
   c. How it affects behavior
   d. How it changes
4. The adequate personality—goal of helping institutions
   a. The theory of self-actualization
   b. What such people are like
   c. How they grow and develop
   d. How inadequacies come about
5. The effect of the physical body on perceiving and behaving
   a. The effect of body structure on perceiving
   b. The basic principles of growth and development
6. The effect of the family and its relationships on the individual's perceptions of self and the world
   a. As source of learning about self and the world
   b. As product and transmitter of culture
   c. The problems of parents in our time
7. The effects of peer relationships on perceptions of self and the world
   a. The principles of group development and functioning
   b. The dynamics of group effects on individuals
8. How people learn
   a. Objective views of learning
   b. Humanistic views of learning
9. The nature of human capacities
   a. The limits of capacities
   b. How these limits develop
   c. How they may be changed
   d. The nature and nurture of creativity
10. The helping relationship
    a. The nature of such relationships

  b. The nature of helpers
  c. How helping relationships are established in a wide variety of settings
11. The nature of communication
  a. The nature and principles of communication
  b. The application of these principles to human interaction

This list of topics might be regarded as an outline for the content of a course in Educational Psychology or in the Psychological Foundations of Education. That, however, would be a great pity! Such topics ought not to be dealt with in a "course." They should be considered and reconsidered repeatedly throughout the student teacher's entire program of training.

To help teachers develop accurate, useful beliefs about children and adults is not a one-shot matter. It requires consideration and reconsideration of the nature of people throughout the student's career and especially during his professional training. The perceptions characteristic of effective teachers are not superficial concepts. They are deeply rooted, ingrained beliefs, buttressed by knowledge, observation, and experience, and they find expression in all aspects of the good teacher's behavior. Such feelings are not acquired quickly or as a consequence of a single course. They come into being through a long slow development involving the confrontation of ideas, to be sure, but even more important, opportunities to discover meanings in interaction with colleagues, students, children, and the physical world.

THE IMPORTANCE OF GENERALIZATIONS

The development of beliefs about people is also not learned from the meaningless accumulation and memorization of minutiae. It is not the details surrounding the topics listed above which teachers need to acquire, but the generalizations and meaning attached to them. The evidence for the principle of maturation, for example, derived from experiments on bladder control or observations of the "ossification of the wrist bones" may be of intense interest to the scholar but contributes very little to the capacity of the practitioner to place the principle into effect.

  Teachers need beliefs and understandings to be applied to particular persons, rather than hundreds of facts about people in the abstract. It is not enough that a teacher know the *facts* about human behavior. Nor is it enough to be able to tell them to someone else or to write out "good" answers on a test paper. The teacher's psychology must be a working psychology, a practitioner's psychology.

One can learn to drive a car even if one is not a mechanic. A mechanic may drive a car better, to be sure, but not enough so as to warrant our taking the time and energy to make mechanics out of all drivers. Similarly, teachers need understanding and application of psychological principles. They do not need to be psychologists. There is a vast difference between understanding a *person* and understanding *about* him.

THE STAFF'S RESPONSIBILITY

For student teachers to acquire the kinds of beliefs characteristic of effective professional workers means that psychology and the problem of the nature of man must be an integral part of the curriculum throughout the college. The responsibility for helping students develop sensitivity cannot be relegated to a particular time, course, or faculty group. Every encounter between students and faculty in or out of the classroom contributes to learning. Students discover their values in interaction with significant people. Despite fine words and lofty sentiments, cynicism, dishonesty, and attitudes of contempt for others will not escape them. In the previous chapter, I pointed out the importance of the attitudes of teachers in the content areas. How much more important it is that the professors that students encounter in the professional aspects of their training should express the kinds of beliefs in people characteristic of effective teachers.

There are professors in teacher-education programs who teach democracy but who don't really believe that "free people can find their own best ways." There are supervisors who don't really think students are able, and administrators so busy dealing with things they forget about persons. I have even seen professors of guidance expressing contempt for the teachers they were sending out counselors to work with. In thinking about teacher-education reform, it is easy to consider courses, regulations, and what to do about students. It is uncomfortable to face the fact that student beliefs are affected by our own. Uncomfortable as it may be, the fact is inescapable. The production of effective teachers is a deeply personal problem, and the humanity and beliefs of the teacher-preparation faculty itself is a crucial factor in the process. Student teachers' beliefs about people are learned from the philosophy and values of their teachers, not just those who teach philosophy and psychology, but all of them, including the dean.

SENSITIVITY AND INVOLVEMENT

One of the characteristics of good teachers from the research reported at the beginning of this chapter is an internal, people-oriented frame of reference, a sensitivity to others. It is this sensitivity which the teacher-education program must develop in its students. Sensitivity is a matter of feelings, beliefs, and understandings, the ability to put oneself in the other fellow's shoes and to see the way things are with him. It is a matter of making inferences about how people think and feel and perceive and of checking these inferences against experience. Knowing a principle is but a first step toward understanding. Sensitivity comes only as students discover the deeper meaning of principles.

Sensitivity is an active thing. It cannot be learned at arm's length. Its development requires active involvement of self with people, the use of the teacher's own being as an instrument, as an observer and maker of inferences about people and their worlds. The development of sensitivity is a matter of commitment. To learn what people are really like, teachers-in-training need the encounter of personal interaction with ideas and with people, both children and adults. This kind of involvement may be brought about by all the ways I have suggested in Chapter 3 and by others which the reader may devise for his own peculiar tasks. Almost any kind of encounter can have important learning values for the student, but, of course, some will be much more fruitful than others.

Perhaps the most time-honored device for developing sensitivity has been the use of observations. Most teacher-education programs require students to spend many hours observing the behavior of students or teachers. Many instructors put great faith in this technique despite the fact that student teachers often find it distasteful and a waste of time. This has long disturbed me, but I find now that applying the principles of perceptual psychology to the problem has helped me see this matter in a new light. I am now convinced that we have often made such experiences fruitless and frustrating for our students because of a mistaken belief that observations must be made objectively.

Many of us have made such a fetish of objectivity in the making of observations that we have blinded students to the real meaning and values of observing. Because we want to develop in students "disciplined observation," to see what is *really* going on, we have insisted that they report exactly what occurred, precisely, and in detail. But one of the factors that determines perception is the intent of the perceiver, and students set to look at behavior in detail dutifully see it so and report it so. They are thus committed to a very dull task. Here, for example, is a portion of a lengthy observation report made by a teacher-in-training:

> Jimmy picked up his pencil, examined the end of it. He saw that it needed sharpening so he got out of his seat and walked to the back of the room. He sharpened his pencil, looked out the window for a moment and returned to his seat. On the way back to his seat, he tapped his friend, Joe, on the head with the pencil as he passed him. He sat down and straightened his paper. He looked at the board where the teacher had placed the problem. He read the problem to himself. He sucked on the end of his pencil. He twisted his feet around the bottom of his desk and then he started to write the answer. He worked very slowly and once in a while he would look up and around the room. Once he put his head down on his arm and wrote from that position. He looked up and saw Ed Price. He made a face at Ed and shrugged his shoulders. . . .

Is it any wonder that students often find this kind of reporting sheer drudgery? It should not surprise us that they rebel at such busywork. But this is not just a waste of time. Worse yet, it directs the student's attention to the wrong issues! For example, if the student is observing a teacher, the need for objectivity focuses his attention on the teacher's behavior or methods. But methods, as we have seen earlier, can never be comprehended as acts in themselves. Without consideration of the teacher's purposes and perceptions of self, students, and situation, objective reporting of what the teacher did is practically useless. Following this procedure, the student fails to understand the teacher on the one hand and looks in the wrong places for his own improvement on the other. Observing a child objectively, the student's attention is directed to behavior rather than causes. This leads naturally to a preoccupation with management rather than helping, controlling rather than facilitating. Children can rarely be understood from a consideration of their behavior alone. It is only as we comprehend its meaning to them that we find the key to working with them.

In the research reported at the beginning of this chapter, effective teachers were found to be internally oriented, concerned with how things seem to the child in the present. It is through this kind of orientation that we must seek understanding and the development of sensitivity.

Seeing the problem in this way, I have given up asking my students to make coldly factual, detailed observation reports. I now ask them to do what I do myself when I watch a child behaving or a teacher teaching—to get the "feel" of what's going on, to see if they can get inside the skin of the person being observed, to understand how things look from his point of view. I ask them, "What do you think he is trying to do?" "How do you suppose he feels?" "How would you have to feel to behave like that?" "How does he see the other kids?" "What does he feel about the subject?" and so on.

What students learn from such experiences can be immeasurably enhanced by effective teaching and supervision. Sensitivity seems most effectively learned when involvement is accompanied by, or followed as closely as possible by, opportunities to explore and consider the meaning of what was experienced. Many instructors are keenly aware of this principle and provide opportunities for the exploration of the meaning of experience through various types of group discussions designed to give students opportunities to kick ideas around and to test them against the interaction of others. Involvement can also be obtained from activities carried out alone, such as an individual research project or the writing of a paper. It may also occur in activities which do not bring people face-to-face. I have experimented in my teaching, for example, with having students write me letters about their reactions to their experiences. These have often proved extremely valuable both to the student and the instructor. Generally speaking, however, various forms of group discussion or individual interaction remain our most valuable means of inducing the exploration and discovery of meaning.

Best results are achieved when it is possible to combine observations with immediate discussion in the excellent fashion described by Sarason[10] or in the kinds of discussion sessions advocated by Earl Kelley.[11] One of the great contributions of television to teacher education is the opportunities it provides to carry on observation and

[10] S. B. Sarason, K. Davidson, and B. Blott, *The Preparation of Teachers* (New York: Wiley, 1962).

[11] E. C. Kelley, *The Workshop Way of Learning* (New York: Harper, 1951).

discussion simultaneously without disturbing teachers or pupils in the process. Whatever the techniques we use, student teachers need every possible help in the exploration and discovery of accurate and workable concepts of what people are like and why they behave as they do. In this chapter we have looked at some of the ways students may be helped to acquire such beliefs from psychology and philosophy, from his experiences with his teachers, and from personal involvement with children and teachers. Beliefs about people are also acquired from the ways in which the student himself is treated, and that is the topic of our next chapter.

6

The Teacher's Self

THE SELF OF THE EFFECTIVE TEACHER

THE ESSENCE OF SUCCESSFUL PROFESSIONAL WORK is the effective use of self. This personal quality of professional training has already been recognized in the training of doctors, counselors, nurses, social workers, pastors, and psychotherapists. It is equally true for the training of teachers. The good teacher is first and foremost a person. The fact of his person-ness is the vehicle through which whatever teaching he does is accomplished.

What is more, the process of learning itself is a matter of personal exploration and discovery. A program of teacher education which has not affected its students in personal ways has failed its mission. The effective teacher must *be* somebody. He is not a passive baby-sitter meekly following instructions, guiding students through steps and processes in which he is not involved. Neither does he hide behind his subject matter and pour out objective facts like a phonograph. Good teaching involves personal interaction. The process of teacher education must be as student-centered as modern philosophy demands the teaching occurring in all our schools should be.

THE CAPACITY FOR SHARING SELF

The production of a professional worker calls for the ability to share self on the one hand and to discipline self on the other. The teacher's willingness and ability to enter into relationships with students, colleagues, and subject matter is crucial to effective teaching. This calls for qualities of openness, of "making one's self visible." The individual must be willing to disclose himself and to permit other people to see him as he is, to know what he thinks, believes, and stands for.

This personal interaction is basic to communication. We do not listen to nonentities and we do not hear light-weights. I have often observed in my classes that communication between me and my students increases in direct proportion to the degree of "earned" authority I hold in their eyes. By "earned" authority, I do not mean my titles or the books I have written. I earned these, to be sure, but not with my students. By "earned" authority, I mean the authority my students invest in me as a consequence of their personal discovery of who I am, what I believe, and whether what I have to say is important. I do not have this earned authority when I meet these students for the first time. All I have then is my "unearned" authority: my degrees, my reputation, and the catalog designation that I am boss of this course. So long as these unearned authorities are in ascendance in our relationship, students hardly hear what I say. Accordingly, they dutifully write things down because if they did not, they would forget them. Later, when they know me better, and if I have earned my place as teacher in their eyes, they do not bother to write much down. We do not forget what *important* people have to say to us.

THE ADEQUATE PERSONALITY

The giving of self called for in helping professions like teaching is probably possible only in the degree to which the helper himself feels basically fulfilled. A deeply deprived self cannot afford to give itself away. A self must possess a satisfactory degree of adequacy before it can venture commitment and encounter. As Earl Kelley has expressed it, people must feel that "they are enough."[1] A small, weak self cannot behave in ways that risk further diminution.

The question of what constitutes an adequate self has intrigued a number of psychologists in recent years. They have tried to discover just what such people would be like. Some of these writers have referred to the "fully functioning self," "self-actualization," "self-realization," "the adequate personality," and "high level wellness." By whatever name they have approached the question, however, all are asking, "What kind of person would it be who was truly achieving the utmost of his potentialities?" In my own explorations I have sought

[1] Earl C. Kelley, "The Fully Functioning Self," in A. W. Combs, ed., *Perceiving, Behaving, Becoming: A New Focus for Education,* 1962 ASCD Yearbook (Washington, D. C.: Association for Supervision and Curriculum Development, 1962).

to approach the question from a perceptual point of view. Looked at in this way, highly adequate personalities seem to be characterized by four general qualities: [2,3]

1. They tend to see themselves in essentially positive ways. That is to say, they see themselves as generally liked, wanted, successful, able persons of dignity, worth, and integrity.
2. They perceive themselves and their world accurately and realistically. These people do not kid themselves. They are able to confront the world with openness and acceptance, seeing both themselves and external events with a minimum of distortion or defensiveness.
3. They have deep feelings of identification with other people. They feel "at one with" large numbers of persons of all kinds and varieties. This is not simply a surface manifestation of "liking people" or being a "hail-fellow-well-met" type of person. Identification is not a matter of polished social graces, but a feeling of oneness in the human condition.
4. They are well informed. Adequate people are not stupid. They have perceptual fields which are rich, varied, and available for use when needed.

In the 1962 ASCD Yearbook, *Perceiving, Behaving, Becoming,*[4] a national committee of educators explored what the concept of the adequate personality meant for educational practice. They came to the conclusion that the production of such persons is the very goal of education and that the above qualities of self-actualization provide important guidelines for educational practice. These criteria are equally important for determining the kinds of teachers we would like to produce. Where else in our society is it more important that adequate persons be in command than in guiding and encouraging youth? Recent research suggests that possessing an adequate personality is directly associated with professional success.

In the field of counseling, it has been found that successful counselors see themselves as more adequate, trustworthy, worthy, wanted, and identified with others than do less successful ones,[5] and an even more recent study comparing good and poor teachers reached similar

[2] A. W. Combs and Donald Snygg, *Individual Behavior* (New York: Harper, 1959).

[3] A. W. Combs, ed., *Perceiving, Behaving, Becoming: A New Focus for Education,* 1962 ASCD Yearbook (Washington, D. C.: Association for Supervision and Curriculum Development, 1962).

[4] *Ibid.*

[5] A. W. Combs and D. W. Soper, "Perceptual Organization of Effective Counselors," *J. Counsel. Psych.,* 1963, **10**, No. 3, 222–226.

conclusions about the way good teachers typically perceive them-selves.[6,7]

1. Good teachers feel identified with, rather than apart from others. The good teacher tends to see himself as a part of all man-kind; he sees himself as identified with people rather than as with-drawn, removed, apart or alienated from others.

2. Good teachers feel basically adequate rather than inadequate. The good teacher generally sees himself as enough; as having what is needed to deal with his problems. He does not see himself as lacking and as unable to cope with problems.

3. Good teachers feel trustworthy rather than untrustworthy. The good teacher has trust in his own organism. He sees himself as essentially dependable, reliable, as having the potentiality for coping with events as opposed to seeing self in a tentative fashion with doubts about the potentiality and reliability of the organism.

4. Good teachers see themselves as wanted rather than unwanted. The good teacher sees himself as essentially likeable, attractive (in personal, not physical appearance sense), wanted, and in general ca-pable of bringing forth a warm response from those people important to him; as opposed to feeling ignored, unwanted, or rejected by others.

5. Good teachers see themselves as worthy rather than unworthy. The good teacher sees himself as a person of consequence, dignity, integrity and worthy of respect; as opposed to being a person of little consequence who can be overlooked, discounted, whose dignity and integrity do not matter.

It is apparent that these characteristics of effective teachers and counselors tally closely with the qualities of the adequate personality indicated above. If these are the characteristics of good teachers, then it follows that these are the perceptual characteristics we need to produce in the professional education of teachers.

THE CAPACITY FOR DISCIPLINING SELF

Although teaching is a deeply personal matter, it is not a self-indulgent one. The purpose of teaching is service; its primary goal is the growth

[6] C. T. Gooding, "An Observational Analysis of the Perceptual Organiza-tion of Effective Teachers," Unpublished Ed.D. Dissertation (Gainesville: Univ. of Florida, 1964).

[7] Deleted.

of self in the student, not the teacher. This is a goal often lost sight of, particularly by college teachers addicted to lecturing. As one of my students put it, commenting on his college frustrations, "I always thought college was for the nourishment of the student, but I was wrong. College exists for the enhancement of the professor!"

While self-disclosure is necessary for communication, self-discipline is equally called for. Good teaching is not maudlin. Teachers must have dignity, integrity, and the capacity to set one's self aside long enough to minister to the needs of others. This is not easy for the beginning teacher. It is a difficult thing to set aside one's own needs. Most of us can do this only for very short periods and then only by dint of considerable conscious, careful effort.

Whether an individual is able to set self aside in the manner required for self-discipline will also depend on the degree of personal adequacy he feels. It is only when persons feel fundamentally adequate that self can be transcended and attention given to the needs of others. Inadequate persons cannot afford the time and effort required to assist others as long as they feel deprived themselves. "Selfishness" is characteristic of maladjustment and inadequacy.

It is a fascinating thing that the necessity for "coping" with life becomes greatly reduced in the experience of adequate persons. Maslow, for example, points out that all of us have two kinds of behaviors: 1) Those things we do in order to cope with life and 2) those kinds of behaviors which are simply expressive, behaviors carried out as fulfillments or expressions of ourselves.[8] Adequate personalities, interestingly enough, show far less coping behavior and much more expressive behavior than other people. Apparently, in simply expressing themselves they manage to deal effectively with the world without the necessity for giving such problems much attention. Just by being who he is, the adequate personality achieves what the inadequate one must work at. Self-discipline is not a conscious effort for such persons but a natural consequence of an internal state. The teacher who feels fundamentally adequate can and will give of himself, automatically, without the necessity for working at it.

In the light of these understandings, the production of good teachers is in part synonymous with the production of more adequate personalities. It follows that teacher-education programs must assist

[8] A. H. Maslow, *Motivation and Personality* (New York: Harper, 1954).

students in every way to greater experiences of self-fulfillment. Programs must be oriented toward the production of at least the criteria for adequacy we have indicated above. In addition to helping students be well informed, which we have always sought, we need further to aid students to perceive themselves in positive ways, to confront themselves and the world with openness and acceptance, and to develop a deep sense of identification in the human condition.

PRODUCING TEACHERS WITH ADEQUATE PERSONALITIES

THE SELECTION PROGRAM

One way of acquiring teachers who see themselves and others in adequate ways is to select them. Everyone has numerous way of seeing himself, acquired from the experience of living. These beliefs may be accurate and helpful or inaccurate and confusing, but no one can operate in the world we live in without some conception of himself and what other people are like. Professional education, then, is not a matter of teaching people to perceive something entirely new and unique. Rather, it is a question of helping people to change the perceptions they already have or to discover new and deeper meanings of already existing concepts. There are some lucky people whose life experiences have already taught them to perceive themselves and others in ways that at the very start are superior to the concepts some of their fellow students will achieve by the end of the program. It is literally true that some people do not need special training to make them good teachers. Unhappily, the number of such persons is quite small and most people still need help. So we shall, no doubt, need teacher-preparation programs for a long time to come.

Theoretically, of course, it is possible to make almost anyone into a good teacher, given the time and the necessary program. Practically, however, the attempt to make just anyone into an effective teacher is too wasteful to consider. A teacher-training program must weigh the cost of its program not only in dollars and cents but also in terms of the most efficient use of the time and energies of its faculty and the time and anguish of its students. The prospects for a teacher-education program might be divided into three groups:

1. Those who already possess a considerable measure of the perceptual qualities of the good teacher we have indicated in these discussions;

2. Those who have a fair degree of these conceptual qualities and who seem likely to profit from professional education;
3. Those who have very little such perceptual organization and seem likely to change only very slowly.

The first of these groups we need to recruit into our profession as rapidly as possible. The third group will require so much time, effort, and expense as to make the task too inefficient. These people should probably be helped to explore other alternatives. From the middle group we need to accept as many as possible, working down from the top until we have filled our facilities to capacity.

The Inadequacy of Objective Data.   Most of us approach the business of selection with a great deal of apprehension. We do not want to hurt people and we are worried that our unsupported human judgments may be inaccurate. As a consequence we usually select students on the basis of indications of academic aptitude derived from past records and tests of academic ability. Some teacher-preparation programs have added to this, very tentatively, judgments about personality and adjustment and even sometimes a personal interview. When these latter criteria have been added, it has usually been with apologies. We feel vaguely guilty using such "nonscientific," subjective criteria even though heavy reliance upon objectively measured criteria boomerangs to destroy the very goals we seek.

We live in a world dominated by the "scientific method." Daily, we are provided with apparent proof of the superiority of controlled measurement over free-wheeling human observation. We are impressed and we have a right to be. Wherever these devices are applicable to our problems, we certainly should use them. But science has become a sacred cow in our generation, and there is a seductive comfort in numbers. It is reassuring to be able to substantiate our own judgments by the apparently infallible statistic or written record. Accordingly, records of past behavior and the results of batteries of tests are given tremendous weight in selecting students. Sometimes, unhappily, they are even used exclusively.

In this book we have been describing the adequate teacher in perceptual terms. Neither records of past behavior nor test results, however, can be relied upon at this stage of our knowledge to provide us with the information we need about human perceptions. Tests of academic aptitude can tell us something about the individual's probable success in acquiring subject matter. They tell us very little about the kinds of perceptual organization we want to know about in judging probable success in teaching.

The Need for Subjective Judgments. Perceptual psychologists are beginning to find out how to explore the nature of perceptions, but we do not yet have simple measuring devices to get at these aspects of human personality. This is an area in which we need a great deal more research. Meantime, if we are to improve our selective processes it will be necessary for us to accept human judgments, values, and feelings as valid data upon which to make decisions. It may be that in doing this we will make some mistakes.[9,10] This need not worry us unduly. Men have always had to proceed on the basis of the very best judgments they could make when they did not have other measures to work with. We may not wish to make such judgments, but we cannot avoid doing so. A professional worker is a person whose judgment can be relied upon. It is this quality of judgment that separates professional work from mechanical. Only the profession can judge the effectiveness of its members.[11] Excluding human judgment and experience from decision-making only compounds the error of accepting objective data uncritically, especially when such data are not really related to our problems. Every profession which deals with human beings must make its most important decisions on the basis of judgments which cannot be set in numerical order. Teaching is a profession dependent upon human values, and these must be accepted as valid data for our operations. In thirty years of teaching and selecting students, I do not recall an instance in which I was disappointed in a student when I let my judgment overrule the statistics. All of my failures in selection have been in those instances when I have succumbed to the belief that the statistics must surely be right and my own judgment wrong.

[9] See G. W. Denemark, ed., *Criteria for Curriculum Decisions in Teacher Education* (Washington, D. C.: Association for Supervision and Curriculum Development, 1964) for an excellent review of the problem of selection and suggestions for selection programs.

[10] Margaret Lindsey, *New Horizons for the Teaching Profession* (Washington, D. C.: National Commission on Teacher Education and Professional Standards, N. E. A., 1961).

[11] A. W. Combs, "Can We Measure Good Teaching Objectively?" *N. E. A. Journal,* 1964, **53,** 34–36+.

I am not advocating that we set aside objective measures completely. We need such measures, but only in their proper place as contributing evidence in the process of selection. The making of professional judgments will never be perfect. But the search for objective criteria is a blind alley, and psychologists are a long way from providing devices for measuring good teaching from a perceptual orientation. Therefore, we have no alternative but to use professional judgment as the best device available at this time. Our selections must be based upon the very best data we are able to gather, but the judgments we finally make must stand with apologies to no one.

CHANGING SELF-PERCEPTIONS

Having selected the most likely prospects, how shall the teacher-training program go about helping students change their ways of seeing themselves? Since the ways in which people see themselves and the world is a purely internal matter, it is clear that one cannot hope to approach the problem directly. It is not a question of telling the student what he must be and do to become an effective teacher. People do not change themselves that way. They arrive at a way of seeing themselves and the world as a consequence of experience. One kind of experience, to be sure, is what we hear and what we read about, but such experience will have very little effect until it is made a part of the self through some experience of one's own.

Personal change is not an objective problem; it is a subjective one. Objective analysis of self has been vastly over-rated as a device for personality change. Effective changes in self are not brought about by picking at the self. This practice can even be highly destructive. Changes in behavior, including changes in one's personality, are most effectively brought about, not by introspection and analysis, but through slow changes in perceptions about outside events and their relation to the self. To produce a change in a person's self requires some new experience which helps him to perceive himself in a different way. This may be brought about in at least three ways:

1. Through some direct provision of experience as, for example, when a child is aided through remedial reading to discover that he really can read, after all, or a student teacher comes to believe he *can* teach as a result of a series of successful experiences;

2. As a consequence of perceiving an event in a new perspective. Some teachers have been so thoroughly indoctrinated with the idea

that children are delicate and anything they do may ruin a child that when they make a mistake in handling a youngster, they are filled with remorse and conclude that they are failures. Helping such teachers understand the really tough character of children and the genesis of maladjustment in more realistic terms permits the teacher to assess himself in more accurate terms.

3. Self-perception may change through interaction following changed perception of others. For example, one does not become more lovable by "deciding" to be or by contemplation of one's own "lovableness." One feels more lovable when the ways one perceives others causes one to behave toward them in such fashion as to touch their hearts so that they react in loving ways. Thus a change in the perception of others causes them to behave in ways that change the self. The self is learned from the looking-glass held up for us by others.

These principles provide us with clues to what the teacher-education program must do to produce more effective concepts of self in its students. Since the self-concept of the teacher is learned in the same fashion as any other perception, the conditions for learning discussed in an earlier chapter are equally relevant here. Teacher educators must concern themselves with

1. Creating an atmosphere in the college and within its classrooms and activities which encourages and facilitates the student's discovery of himself as a more adequate person and teacher;
2. Providing experiences designed to help students see themselves as adequate effective people;
3. Assisting actively the student's personal search for meaning and the discovery of himself as a person and as a teacher.

Within the framework for learning, what kinds of experiences shall educators provide in order to assure the development of adequate and effective teachers? The guidelines are plainly set before us. They may be found in current thinking about the nature of the adequate person and in the research on good teaching mentioned earlier in this chapter.

Adequate personalities, say the perceptual psychologists, are people who see themselves in positive ways: as liked, wanted, acceptable, and able. So do good teachers. But these definitions of desirable perceptual qualities are more than definitions of goodness. They provide the criteria in terms of which we may select the kinds of experiences we need in order to produce more adequate teachers.

If it is true that good teachers see themselves as liked, wanted, acceptable, and able, then these are the kind of personal perceptions the teacher-education program must produce. And the way it is done is to treat students so. People learn that they are liked, wanted, acceptable, and able from experiences of having been treated that way by the people around them and from successful experiences which teach them they are able. Teacher-education students take their self-concepts with them wherever they go and every experience they have makes its contribution pro or con in building or tearing down self-perceptions.[12,13] Helping to build up students' self-concepts is a responsibility of every member of the teacher-preparation faculty. It cannot be set aside as the exclusive task of any special group. Each staff member has his effect upon the self-concepts of students whether he wants to or not. The only thing he can control is whether his impact on the student will be positive, negative, or of no account whatever.

In similar fashion, the attitudes of self-acceptance and openness to experience, characteristic of adequate persons and effective teachers, are the consequence of successful experiences in this realm. One learns to accept oneself from having been accepted by significant people. Openness to experience is learned in part from positive feelings about self which make risk-taking possible and partly from association with open, courageous persons. A teacher-preparation faculty is no place for timid souls.

So, too, feelings of commitment, encounter, and oneness in the human condition are learned in the process of growing up from those around us. It follows that teacher educators must contribute to student feelings of belonging and must provide an atmosphere of compassion and concern for people from which feelings of identification can be acquired.

The characteristics of adequate personalities and the perceptual characteristics of effective professional workers are not inherent qualities. They are learned and what is learned can be taught. Research on the nature of adequacy has pointed the way. It remains for

[12] P. E. McClendon, "Teacher Perception and Working Climate," *Ed. Leadership*, 1962, **20**, 104–109.

[13] W. W. Lynch, "Person Perception: Its Role in Teaching," *Indiana Univ. School of Ed. Bull.*, 1961, **37**, 1–37.

teacher educators to set about the business of achieving such ways of seeing self in our students with greater efficiency if we are to meet our responsibilities to the next generations.

How shall we do it? For this author to attempt to spell out in detail what needs to be done in order to put these principles into effect would be presumptuous indeed. This is not an objective to be assigned to a particular course. Nor is it a matter for any individual to decide. It is a matter for education faculties to address themselves to in whatever ways are appropriate in the light of their local purposes and conditions. It must involve all aspects of the program and all members of the staff, beginning with a belief that "people are important," then formulating plans and procedures to provide the kinds of experiences which will assure the production of teachers with the perceptual organization of effective professional workers. In the characteristics of the adequate personality outlined for us by perceptual psychology, and in the research on the nature of the self of good teachers, we have a yardstick for a critical appraisal of current practices on the one hand and guidelines for the development of new practices on the other.

A good beginning in this direction has already been suggested in the 1962 ASCD Yearbook, *Perceiving, Behaving, Becoming.*[14] In this volume the committee of teachers who wrote the yearbook have systematically examined educational practices which impede or encourage 1) the positive view of self, 2) self-acceptance and the accurate view of self, 3) creativity and openness to experience, and 4) the feeling of identification. The work of these educators has already attracted much attention among public-school teachers and curriculum workers. Most of what they have to say is equally applicable to problems of teacher education. Their thinking can serve as an effective starting place for any college faculty interested in building an improved program for the professional training of teachers.

THE STUDENT COUNSELING PROGRAM

A professional program oriented around the personality of the teacher must maintain steady contact with its students. If teachers-in-training are to take greater responsibilities for their own learning, and if the learning program is to be continually adjusted to student readiness,

[14] A. W. Combs, *Perceiving, Behaving, Becoming,* Chapters 8, 9, 10, 11.

machinery must be established to provide for the kind of personal contact which will make such a program possible. This calls for an effective counseling program.[15] It would be ideal if all members of the faculty could do a good job of counseling with students and would regard this as an important aspect of their jobs. Such a millennium, however, has not yet been reached, and it is probably unrealistic to expect this of any faculty. What is needed is to make adjustments in terms of faculty responsibilities, competencies, and interests with respect to counseling so as to make the most effective use of those who possess counseling talents.

A professional program oriented around student growth will need to help students continually to review, evaluate, and plan for further activities. This kind of personal interest should be provided for all students. It can best be given by those members of the staff who have continuing contacts with students and who like this kind of personal contact, those who can take an interest in students and relate to them in warm and friendly fashion. The training of a counselor is not a mysterious laying-on-of-hands procedure. It is a matter of helping an individual to make effective use of himself in face-to-face relationships. Good teachers usually make good counselors. Beginning with such personnel, the counseling procedures of any teacher-education program can often be greatly improved by a comparatively simple course of in-service training. All that is needed is an instructor who knows his business and who is interested in improving his techniques and understanding in the field of counseling.

Since the making of a teacher is a highly personal thing, the teacher-preparation counseling program also needs to give more intensive personal counseling than that ordinarily provided by instructors and advisers. A student's capacity to use himself as an effective instrument will depend in large part on his personal happiness and freedom from psychological distress. There is ample reason for advocating a program of counseling for students solely on the basis of its desirability for personal and human reasons. It is even more desirable in professional education. In a business like teaching, above all, we need adequate, healthy personalities, and it is a responsibility of the teacher-training institution to bring about this end as effectively and as positively as it can. There is ample evidence to demonstrate a relationship between the mental health of teachers and students. But even if this

[15] Denemark, *op cit.*

were not so, the effect of unhappiness and inadequacy on the sheer productivity and efficiency of teachers should be enough to convince us of the importance of personal counseling during the student's training days.

The provision of personal counseling for students is, of course, expensive. Schools are also hesitant at times to assume responsibility for this aspect of the student's life. It is often argued that in a society not yet ready to assume the financial burdens of this kind of service, the college can accept only very limited responsibility for the personal adjustment of students. This argument may have some validity in the training of engineers, physicists, mathematicians, and scholars in the various disciplines. Surely it does not apply in the preparation of teachers, the people to whom we entrust major responsibility for the health and welfare of our youth. A profession whose business is to produce adequate people must ensure that its ranks are filled by people who can carry out that responsibility and who are themselves the most adequate people we can find. The personal qualities of the teacher are so important that a professional training program must either help its students to become the most effective people they can be or help them to leave the profession as gracefully as possible. A professional program which ignores this facet of training must necessarily be less efficient than is desirable.

Fortunately, not all students need personal counseling. One of the tasks of an effective selection system should be to make certain of the basic health of students entering the program. If selection is effective, a teacher-education program should not be saddled with very many cases requiring deep counseling. Most personal counseling does not require extensive psychiatric service. While any school will, of course, have occasional students who need deep psychiatric care, the vast majority can be helped by counseling of a much less intensive sort. Nonmedical counselors of very high quality are now being produced in increasing numbers by schools of social work, psychology, counseling, and guidance. The presence of counselors on a college staff can often make important contributions to the program in other than their purely counseling roles. In fact, it is probably unwise to assign counselors to full-time counseling practice. It is much better to utilize the many important teaching functions which can be carried out by such personnel for part of their time so that they become recognized as an integral part of the faculty.

7

The Teacher's Purposes

ANOTHER FACTOR IN THE PRODUCTION OF AN EFFECTIVE TEACHER has to do with his purposes. Teachers like everyone else behave in terms of what seems important to them. Human behavior is always purposeful. In fact, the purposes driving individuals are so fundamental that they give color and direction to personality itself. Offer me two tickets to the symphony concert and how I behave with respect to your offer will depend on what seems important to me. Each of the following purposes, for example, will produce a quite different behavior on my part:

1. I like symphony music;
2. I dislike symphony music;
3. I do not want to be obligated to you;
4. I have another engagement for that evening;
5. I need $5 badly and know where I could sell the tickets;
6. There is a movie I have been waiting to see that very same evening;
7. My wife has an engagement that evening and I do not want to go alone; and so on.

The possibilities are almost endless. Personality itself is a consequence of our purposes, and the behaviors produced from them make it possible for others to "read" our personalities. All of us are sensitive to the purposes of other people, as when we say of another person, "Well, he would!"

How teachers behave in the classroom, the faculty meeting, the teachers' convention, or sitting at home before the television is determined by the purposes they seek to fulfill in each instance. In Chapter 1 we defined the effective teacher as one who has learned to use himself effectively in carrying out his own and society's purposes. The teacher who is confused about what he is trying to do creates

82

confusion in his students and is very likely to fail in accomplishing either his own or society's objectives.

When purposes are confused or misdirected, behavior is too. Worse still, confusion of purpose makes it almost impossible for other people to deal with the teacher and is an important cause of teacher failure. Students can, after all, only deal with a teacher in terms of the expectancies they have come to feel are characteristic of him. If the teacher's values and purposes are confused, then the student is left groping around in the dark in his attempt to find a way of working effectively with his teacher. To avoid this kind of confusion, young teachers have often been admonished to "be consistent." Such advice is seldom likely to be helpful, however, because it is directed to the wrong goal. Consistency does not lie in the repetitive character of behavior. It is a function of the stability and clarity of the individual's beliefs about what is important and worth doing.

The ways in which a teacher behaves in the classroom, his very methods, will be affected by his purposes and the beliefs he holds about what is truly important. For example, what the teacher does when the class routine is suddenly interrupted by a child falling out of his chair will be quite different depending upon which of the following he feels is important:

1. To get on with the lesson;
2. To save face before the class;
3. To demonstrate his own power and control;
4. To "teach the child a lesson";
5. To save the child embarrassment;
6. To take a break from the concentration on the lesson;
7. To teach good manners; and so on.

The beliefs teachers hold about what is important determine what they respond to and what methods they choose to deal with matters. Good teaching calls for healthy purposes capable of producing behavior in the best interests of everyone: teacher, pupil, and society itself.

Even the society's or the administration's purposes can only be given effective expression if, somehow, they have become a part of the personal purposes of the teacher, for it is only personal purposes that are likely to find their way into expression in the classroom situation. Many an administrator or supervisor seeking to bring about changes in teaching has discovered this fact with annoyance and frustration. No matter how well a teacher may have learned to give the "right" answers and say the "right" things, when the classroom door is shut there is no one but the pupils and the teacher to decide what is to be done. Under these conditions, unless the teacher has made the administration's or society's purposes his own, it is almost certain they will not be carried out. The only way we can be sure teachers will carry out the community's purposes is to find ways of helping teachers develop commitment to them.

THE PURPOSES OF EFFECTIVE TEACHERS

What kinds of purposes do good teachers seek fulfillment for? As with human beings generally, teachers' purposes vary greatly from person to person. Some will be as specific as "writing this question on the board." Others will be more general, like "helping children develop to the maximum of their potentialities." Some will be quite social and philosophical, like "understanding democracy." Still others will be highly individual, as, for example, "helping Jimmy Smith catch up in reading" or personal, as when a teacher says, "It makes me feel so good when I've found a way to teach it better." We have already seen that teaching is a unique expression of a particular personality and that the search for common ways of behaving is probably fruitless. But purposes are ways of perceiving, and research has already demonstrated that good professional workers perceive in common ways about themselves and others. Research has also demonstrated that good professional workers can be discriminated from poor ones on the basis of purposes in at least two other professions. The purposes of effective counselors, for example, have been found to be

1. Self-revealing rather than self-concealing;
2. "Freeing" rather than "controlling";
3. Altruistic rather narcissistic;
4. Concerned with larger goals rather than smaller ones.[1]

Similarly, effective Episcopal priests were found to have purposes described as freeing rather than controlling; becoming involved rather than avoiding involvement.[2]

---

[1] A. W. Combs and D. W. Soper, "Perceptual Organization of Effective Counselors," *J. Counsel. Psych.*, 1963, **10**, No. 3, 222–226.

[2] John A. Benton, "Perceptual Characteristics of Episcopal Pastors," Unpublished Ed.D. Dissertation (Gainesville: Univ. of Florida, 1964).

Recent research has also shown that effective teaching is, in part, the product of certain kinds of purposes. Good and poor teachers, for example, can be distinguished with respect to the following kinds of purposes:[3,4]

1. Good teachers perceive their purpose in teaching as being one of freeing, rather than controlling, students. That is to say, the teacher perceives the purpose of the helping task as one of freeing, assisting, releasing, facilitating, rather than as a matter of controlling, manipulating, coercing, blocking, or inhibiting behavior.

2. Good teachers tend to be more concerned with larger rather than smaller issues. They tend to view events in a broad rather than a narrow perspective. They are concerned with the broad connotations of events, with larger, more extensive implications, rather than with the immediate and specific. They are not exclusively concerned with details but can perceive beyond the immediate to the future.

3. Good teachers are more likely to be self-revealing than self-concealing. They are willing to disclose self. They can treat their feelings and shortcomings as important and significant rather than hiding or covering them up. They seem willing to be themselves.

4. Good teachers tend to be personally involved rather than alienated. The teacher sees his appropriate role as one of commitment to the helping process, a willingness to enter into interaction, as opposed to being inert or remaining aloof or remote from action.

5. Good teachers are concerned with furthering processes rather than achieving goals. They seem to see their appropriate role as one of encouraging and facilitating the process of search and discovery as opposed to promoting or working for a personal goal or a preconceived solution.

Other characteristics with respect to the teacher's purposes have been suggested as connected with good teaching, but have not yet been subjected to research:[5] Good teachers' purposes are those of

1. Helping rather than dominating;
2. Understanding, rather than condemning;

---

[3] C. T. Gooding, "An Observational Analysis of the Perceptual Organization of Effective Teachers," Unpublished Ed.D. Dissertation (Gainesville: Univ. of Florida, 1964).

[4] Deleted.

[5] A. W. Combs, "The Personal Approach to Good Teaching," *Ed. Leadership*, 1964, **21**, 369–378.

3. Accepting rather than rejecting;
4. Valuing integrity rather than violating integrity;
5. Being positive rather than negative;
6. Being open rather than closed to experience;
7. Being tolerant of ambiguity rather than intolerant.

All of the characteristics of effective helpers indicated in the research mentioned above are broad categories of purposes. Within each of these there is room for the individual to find his own more specific ones. If such purposes are truly characteristic of the helping professions, as these researches seem to suggest, they also provide us with important clues as to what needs to be done in the teacher-training program. Somehow we shall have to find ways of involving our students in active consideration of their own and society's purposes.

THE INADEQUACY OF FORMAL COURSES FOR DISCOVERING PURPOSE

Most teacher-training programs recognize the importance of a study of purposes, and they include this study in their programs in courses with such titles as the Philosophy of Education, School and Society, the Social Foundations of Education, the American School. Unhappily, these courses have often failed to accomplish their objectives in anything like the degree we had hoped. The teacher who has not been exposed to classes designed to teach him about democracy in the course of his professional preparation would be rare indeed. Nevertheless, the failure of teachers to understand and apply the principles of democracy in the classroom is the despair of teacher educators everywhere. It is apparent that the mere exposure of people to ideas is by no means a guarantee that they will espouse them.

The formal study of philosophy in most teacher-preparation programs has been disappointing in its effect upon teacher behavior. The same is true with respect to the formal teaching of social foundations. Surely, teachers need an understanding of the social order and its relationship to the history and problems of man and society. Why is it that these topics, so obviously necessary and logically desirable, have generally failed to produce the kinds of results we expected?

Three factors seem to me to be primarily responsible for this state of affairs:

1. The Attempt to "Give" Students Philosophy. As we have seen in Chapter 3, there is a vast difference between knowing and behaving. Abstract ideas do not affect behavior until the behaver has discovered their personal meaning for him. This principle is nowhere more important than in the problem of the teaching of purposes. The development of a philosophy is neither a formal matter nor a descriptive matter. It must be a dynamic problem of personal discovery.

It is now clear that many of our failures in teaching philosophy are a consequence of having put the cart before the horse. We have tried to teach the structure in the absence of experience. The formality of structure and principle is only effective as it follows experience. It cannot substitute for it. Human purposes are not *taught to* people. They cannot be given. They must *emerge from* people. One does not learn John Dewey's philosophy and apply it. One discovers John Dewey's philosophy in one's own purposes and activities. That is a highly personal matter. When social purposes and philosophy are taught as a subject, students may never discover their meanings and never perceive that the information they so carefully learned and wrote about on examinations has anything to do with everyday problems of classroom operations.

2. The Seduction of Language. The principles of philosophy, sociology, and anthropology are concepts extracted from experience and formulated for handy use in dealing with further experience. The attempt to teach such concepts in the absence of experience forces both teacher and student to deal with these matters in purely verbal terms. Instead of developing a personal philosophy, students and teachers are seduced into examining philosophies at arm's length. The words and concepts become important for themselves. Each of the social sciences has developed a court language of its own, like the ancient knight's "language of chivalry" to be used in jousting and tournaments. There is a prestigious "in-group" quality to such language, and it is easy for students and professors to be carried away by it. Higher education is overwhelmingly verbal, and having fun with words is one of the delights of the teaching profession. Unhappily, this may sometimes be carried so far that the ability to speak the language with elegance may come to take the place of learning.

As we have already seen, there is a vast difference between knowing and behaving. The confrontation of varied points of view or even the ability to talk about them well is no guarantee that they will be put to use in the classroom. If it were true that knowing about philosophies is the road to developing one's own, then there should be no more effective personalities on any campus than our professors of philosophy. Unfortunately, this cannot be counted upon. In fact, it is a common student complaint that some teachers who know most about philosophies often seem to behave as though they had none of their own!

3. The Course Organization of Content. Teacher preparation programs have long been addicted to the learn-first—apply-later approach to professional training. The teaching of social and philosophical foundations is no exception. In most places these are still dealt with in some kind of formal course organization. The attempt to teach these vital matters as courses is most inappropriate. Such compartmentalization of knowledge is contrary to what the teacher-education program should be attempting to do. The understanding of society's purposes and the development of one's own system of beliefs are not matters to be formally taught for three hours' credit. The attempt to do so only contributes further to the student's feeling that what he learns in class has little or nothing to do with the practice of his profession.

The course organization of content may have been appropriate to the goals of the liberal arts college from which it was adopted. It is not appropriate for the teacher-preparation program charged with the holistic task of professional training. The social and philosophical purposes of education are not abstract questions. They must be involved in every aspect of preparation of teachers, not as separate notions, but as working guidelines for every teaching act.

THE PROBLEMS APPROACH TO DISCOVERING PURPOSES

Purposes lie inside individuals and cannot be given to them. The teacher-preparation program can only provide the opportunities and conditions in which purposes can be explored and their personal meanings discovered. To do this effectively we must apply the same conditions for learning that we have already advocated for exploring the self in the previous chapter. We must seek continual involvement of students in activities that will spur them to question purposes and goals and that provide opportunities for the students to explore and think about them. Learning will come about as a consequence of the students finding personal answers to such questions as

1. What is really important?
2. What am I trying to do?
3. What do school and society want of me?
4. What do I really want out of teaching?
5. Is what I want worthwhile?
6. Are the things I am doing fulfilling my purposes?
7. Are there better, more important, purposes that I might turn my attention to?
8. Whose purposes are most important here?

It is probable that some variation of the problems approach to teaching is most likely to result in the kind of personal discovery required for the development of effective teachers. Instead of presenting the student with the principles of the topic and asking him to apply them to himself as the usual course organization does, the problems approach tries to help the student extract the principles from his own experience or as a consequence of confrontation with important problems. It attempts to challenge and stimulate students to ask new questions and acquire new knowledge. It involves the student simultaneously in new experiences and in active consideration of their meaning both for himself and for the society of which he is part.

The production of this kind of experience for students also calls for a program extending beyond the one-shot concept of the usual course structure. The exploration and discovery of one's own and society's purposes is not learned in a single exposure. It is a growth process which ought to continue throughout the life of a teacher. It cannot, therefore, be relegated in the teacher-education program to a single course. Effective provisions for its accomplishment must exist throughout the entire teacher-training experience.

The problems approach calls for involving the student in all the ways we suggested in Chapter 3. It asks him not simply to get his feet wet in the profession, but to immerse himself in the problems, practices, and ideas about teaching in every way he can. At the same time, the program is designed to encourage and assist him in exploring and discovering the meaning of all this through contemplation of his experiences. It attempts to keep him continuously engaged in an alternation of practice and exploration, of getting into predicaments and figuring how to get out of them, of watching and thinking, of trying and talking, of making mistakes and trying again. Out of this kind of confrontation with problems and the continuous search for Why? What for? What is good? What works? What is important? What do I believe? purposes and principles become formulated in ways that can later be counted upon to make a difference in how the teacher behaves.

A NEW ORGANIZATION OF SUBJECT MATTER

One of the things almost certain to happen as a result of the problems approach to the teaching of purposes will be the disappearance of psychology, sociology, philosophy, and anthropology as separate and distinct subject areas. This need not disturb us. There is plenty of time for students to tackle the formal disciplines of these subjects if they wish to do so later. Beginning students need experience; advanced students need organization and system. A college student is often but a beginner in many areas of experience despite his adult appearance. "Advancedness" is not a question of age or year in college. It is a matter of experience with problems. Most beginning teachers are no more ready to examine the formal aspects of philosophy, sociology, anthropology, or psychology than the fourth-grade child is to deal with the theory of grammar or the beauties of topological mathematics. These subjects only become separate matters in abstract study. In life situations they are inextricably intertwined. They are experienced simultaneously but formally studied individually. There is already under way in colleges a movement to place formal courses in these subjects at the graduate level; this move seems a good one.

There is another reason why we need not be unduly disturbed at the intermingling of the various social sciences. Increasingly we are coming to recognize that each of the social sciences is but a different way of looking at the same problem—the nature and behavior of human beings. On some campuses there is even a strong movement to combine these groups into single departments of "human relations." This move is often resisted by professors fearful of losing their identity, but despite opposition the idea continues to find increasing favor. The unity of the social sciences as they bear on professional tasks has been recognized by many teacher-education programs in the formation of departments of "educational foundations" that include all the disciplines of the social sciences. Unfortunately, the unity sought by placing these subjects under the same roof has all too often not come about. In most places we continue to deal with purposes, people, and culture as though these were somehow still separate and distinct. The basic objective, however, seems educationally sound, at least insofar as the undergraduate sequence in professional training is concerned. We need to continue searching for ways to make it work.

TWO KINDS OF TEACHERS FOR PROFESSIONAL EDUCATION

To assist students in discovering their own and society's purposes through the problems approach, we must have one of the following:

1. Professors who are highly competent in all the social, philosophical, psychological disciplines and also highly skilled in discussion approaches to teaching through which students can be helped to explore and discover personal meaning. If such people are to be found in the same skin, they must surely be very rare. It seems unlikely that we shall be able to find many in the near future.

2. The alternative seems to call for some kind of team operation which would bring together resource persons from the various foundations disciplines with persons skilled in discussion leadership and the curricular aspects of teaching. The specific combinations of such persons would depend on the peculiar staff talents available in a given college and the degree of flexibility of operations possible.

To implement such a program will not be easy in most colleges because it runs head-on into rigid job descriptions by which most faculties are chosen. Once established, these job descriptions are jealously guarded even when they no longer have relevance or meaning. Job descriptions assume that human talent is entirely organized around content or "knowledge of the subject." One finds everywhere hundreds of articles written on the role of the teacher, or counselor, or principal, or visiting teacher, or school psychologist, and so on, as though these roles could really be defined by prescriptions instead of by people and their behavior. The assumption that beginning teachers can only be taught philosophy, psychology, sociology, aesthetics, or curriculum by experts in these fields is simply not true without reference to the level at which the problems are to be confronted. Roles defined in terms of content are only valid if content is the only question with which we are concerned.

Beginning students need to get acquainted with problems and to explore where these problems may take them. This calls for a kind of instructor who may not be a content specialist but, like the elementary teacher, an expert in encouraging and assisting the processes of learning. Teaming such persons with the content experts would provide both information and exploration aspects needed for the problems approach. A number of colleges have already been experimenting with procedures of this sort with excellent results. Among these are the University of Florida,[6] San Francisco State College,[7] the Project I studies at Rochester, Cornell, Buffalo, and Syracuse universities,[8] and Florida Atlantic University.[9] All of them attempt to involve students deeply in professional matters and each has experimented with various ways of providing students with rich experiences in content as well as opportunities to explore and discover its meaning in seminars or discussion groups under the supervision of trained leaders.

THE USE OF DISCUSSION GROUPS FOR EXPLORATION OF PURPOSES

The use of discussion groups has become an increasingly popular method of instruction in many teacher-preparation programs. In some it is even used almost exclusively while other methods are regarded with much disdain by the faculty. There is no doubt that

[6] I. J. Gordon, J. E. Blackburn, R. L. Curran, D. S. Laird, and W. Olson, "The Florida Experiment in Undergraduate Teacher Education," in *Changes in Teacher Education* (Washington, D. C.: National Commission on Teacher Education and Professional Standards, N. E. A., 1963).

[7] F. T. Wilhelms and A. E. Siemons, "A Curriculum for Personal and Professional Development," in *Changes in Teacher Education* (Washington, D. C.: National Commission on Teacher Education and Professional Standards, N. E. A., 1963).

[8] W. L. Irvine, "Project I: An Experimental Program for the Preparation of Secondary School Teachers," in *Changes in Teacher Education* (Washington, D. C.: National Commission on Teacher Education and Professional Standards, N. E. A., 1963).

[9] Simmons Ballard, in *Program Announcement, 1964–65* (Boca Raton, Fla.: College of Education, Florida Atlantic Univ., 1964).

well-run discussion groups can provide valuable experiences for students. The interaction involved in such groups lends itself especially well to the exploration and clarification of personal purposes. Like any other method of teaching, however, groups are no panacea. What students get out of them varies greatly. They can be exciting and fruitful or downright dull and banal, depending very largely upon the skill of the leaders.

Some of the failures of discussion groups to live up to expectations seem to be due to a confusion between two quite different kinds of discussion groups. Each of these has important values, which unfortunately are often dissipated or destroyed by otherwise skillful instructors who are not aware of the differences between these two kinds of groups and so use them inappropriately.

THE DECISION GROUP

One approach to group discussion might be called the "decision group." Here the purpose is to explore a problem and arrive at some kind of decision about it. In the course of acting in the decision group, members may learn a great deal about the problem under observation. This group is also a kind of small scale model of what our democratic government is like. As a consequence, such groups are popular with instructors concerned about "educating for democracy."

As a means of helping members discuss issues and arrive at group decisions, the decision group has immense value. As a technique for inducing learning and the exploration of purposes, however, it has some serious limitations. The decision group is focused on group action and its goal is arriving at a decision. But learning is an individual matter, and this objective may actually impede effective learning.

The moment a group is required to come to some kind of decision, it begins to operate in ways that coerce its members. It tends, therefore, to cut short individual exploration and discovery in favor of arriving at a group decision. In a decision group there inevitably comes a time when the members who have arrived at a decision begin to put pressure on those who have not. This coercion may be applied with great gentleness so that people are not even conscious of what is happening to them. One way to clothe the iron hand with a velvet glove is to call for a vote. Despite the general acceptance of the vote as a veritable symbol of democracy, it is nevertheless a coercive device of great power, especially on those in the minority. As one of my students expressed it, "A vote is only a means of stopping a discussion." People can be forced to participate, but involvement is another matter requiring an act of will on the part of the person. There is an important place for the decision group in education, but as a technique for inducing effective learning it leaves something to be desired.

THE LEARNING GROUP

The second type of group I have called the "learning group." Its purpose is to allow members to explore and discover ideas and their personal meanings. Since the exploration and discovery of meaning is a purely personal goal, there is no need in such a group for a group decision and, hence, no coercion of individual members. It is even conceivable that there might be less agreement at the end of the discussion than at the beginning. The atmosphere in a learning group is one of mutual assistance and interaction in a setting which respects the dignity and integrity of individuals.

To help students in my classes at the University of Florida use such groups more effectively, we have devised a set of suggestions describing learning groups and how to get the most out of them. I include it here as a thumbnail description of learning groups for interested readers.

GROUP DISCUSSION SUGGESTIONS

What Is a Group Discussion?

It is easy for a group of people to engage in talk but this does not mean that they are having a group discussion. A group discussion is not a debate. Neither is it a bull session. The purpose of a debate is to convince other people of the rightness of one's own position. "Convincing" may even proceed without any real regard for accuracy, but only with a desire to win the argument irrespective of the merits of the position. A bull session, on the other hand, is a pleasant sort of pastime in which one seeks to regale others by descriptions or stories of things he knows or events which have happened to him. Bull sessions are a kind of friendly game of "one-upmanship" in which one person tells a story and the next seeks to top it with still another. Good group discussions are neither of these. The purpose of group discussion is neither to win an argument nor to amuse oneself. Its purpose is to explore and discover personal meanings.

There are two kinds of group discussions in general use in teaching.

One of these is the decision group, in which the primary purpose is to arrive at a consensus or decision on some matter. Almost everyone is familiar with such groups and has participated in them at one time or another. Decision groups can be very helpful in bringing about an agreement on a plan of action. Unfortunately, they may also interfere with the freedom of the individual to explore and move in directions unique to his own needs, for decision groups have the unhappy effect of coercing their members to arrive at the approved solutions.

A second type of discussion group is the "exploratory" or "learning" group. In these sessions the purpose is not to arrive at decisions, but to help each member explore ideas and discover meanings through interaction with other people. Much of our everyday talk is made up of description in which we seek in one way or another to convey ideas to other people. It is usually concerned with what we know. It proceeds with such expressions as "I saw," "I said," "He told me," "There was," etc. A learning group discussion is far more tentative, even halting, in its progress, for it deals not with certainty but with search. It is an exploration of feelings, beliefs, doubts, fears, and concerns. Listening to a group discussion, one is likely to hear such expressions as "It seems to me," "I'm not sure about this but," "Sometimes I wonder if," "What do you think about?," "I think," "I believe," "I wish," and even sometimes if a group feels very safe with each other, "I'm afraid," "I'm angry about" or "I love." Group discussion does not seek to convince. Rather, it deals with matters unsolved and seeks to help each member find meanings not existing before.

A good group discussion is not brought about simply by bringing a group of people together to talk. Good groups take time to form and it is only as the members of a group discover each other as warm, friendly people over a period of time that good group discussion can come about. The following are some suggestions which may help you to make your group a more profitable one for all concerned.

General Considerations

1. For good thinking there must be a sense of relaxation. Group discussion should always be leisurely, not desultory or wandering, but also not hastened or tense. It is more important to think slowly and thoroughly than to cover any prearranged amount of material.

2. Although we hope that all members of our groups will feel free to contribute to the discussion and will want to share their thinking with others, we also recognize that for some people this is a difficult and trying thing to do. No one in our groups is under compulsion to speak. Participation is not measured by words spoken and a silent person may be participating more than his more verbal colleagues.

3. The purpose of the group discussion is the discovery of personal meaning. This calls for "kicking ideas around," testing them, "trying them on for size," examining, comparing, thinking about and talking about ideas until they fit the particular needs and being of each person. This is best accomplished when group members are willing to express their own think-

ing, beliefs, and feelings freely on the one hand and to listen receptively and sympathetically to other people's ideas.

4. Sometimes in a group discussion there may be periods of silence. These need not cause concern. They are a normal function of group discussion which occur at points when a group is thinking deeply, is in process of shifting gears or has exhausted a particular question.

5. Group discussion proceeds best in an atmosphere of warmth and friendliness. Nothing causes people to clam up quicker than being threatened, ridiculed, or humiliated. An atmosphere of acceptance and an honest seeking for understanding is most conducive to good group operation. The more quickly you can get to know and appreciate your fellow group members as individual people, the more quickly your group will begin to pay dividends in growth and development of its members.

Some Specific Suggestions to Group Members

1. Maintain an attitude of searching for a solution. You are trying to find the best answer; not trying to convince other people. Try not to let your previously held ideas interfere with your freedom of thinking. Be on guard against the effect of your own prejudices. You will find this difficult but highly rewarding.

2. Speak whenever you feel moved to do so (and have the right of way, of course) even though your idea may seem incomplete. If the answers were all known, there would be no point in exploring.

3. Cultivate the art of careful listening. You can practice this by trying to formulate in your own mind the gist of what a previous speaker has been saying before adding your own contribution.

4. Try to stay with the group. Discussion which strays too far afield may kill the topic at hand. Avoid introducing new issues until the decks are clean of the business under discussion.

5. Talk briefly. Saying too much may cause people's minds to wander so that they miss the value of what you wish to express.

6. Avoid long stories, anecdotes, or case studies which only illustrate a point. It is ideas, beliefs, implications, and understandings which are the meat of a discussion. Listening to one person after another tell long tales of "what happened to me" can quickly destroy a good discussion.

7. Be as sympathetic and understanding of other people's views as you can. If you disagree, say so, but avoid the appearance of being belligerent or threatening other people.

Ground Rules for Our Discussions

1. Cross examination of other speakers is not permitted. Remember that a group discussion is neither a debate nor a trial. The object is to explore one's own thinking in interaction with others, so we have made it a rule that group members may not ask questions of other group members which smack of cross questioning or which might prove embarrassing. When you feel the urge to cross question another, try instead expressing what you believe and inviting comment and criticism about that.

2. Traffic rules. Speak whenever you feel moved to do so without seeking recognition so long as the track is clear. However, whenever the traffic gets heavy and more than one person seeks to speak at once, then look to the leader to direct the traffic and seek recognition before speaking.

3. A group discussion can only operate well when all members are concerned with the issues before the house. We have therefore made a rule to restrict side conversations to a minimum. Do not hold lengthy conversations with your neighbors, as this forms new groups and destroys the cohesiveness of the total group. Besides, it isn't very well mannered.

8

The Personal Discovery of Ways to Teach

As WE HAVE SEEN IN THE EARLY CHAPTERS OF THIS BOOK, the search for methods of teaching which are "good" or "right" in themselves is fruitless. Modern psychology tells us that methods are but ways of accomplishing purposes. They are not good or bad, right or wrong, by nature. They are vehicles for achieving results. Whether their effects on others are good or bad depends on who is running the vehicle, what he is trying to do, and how this is perceived by those he is doing it to. This personal approach to the problem of methods helps us to understand why so much of our former "logical" approaches to teaching did not produce the results we so earnestly hoped for. And looking at methods in this way, one may see new directions for attention and experimentation which hold promise for more efficient production of the kinds of teachers we so desperately need.

Part of our former difficulty in respect to teaching techniques came about because we tried to find "general" methods, ways of operating that would get results "across the board." Many educators still do. They keep hoping for methods that will work in all times and places and for every variety of teacher. They gather round some methods like political party banners and will fight to the death for hetero-geneous grouping, the self-contained classroom, team teaching, phonics, or the particular fad which happens to be in vogue at the time. But skill in teaching, as we now know, is not a mechanical matter of using the right methods at the right time. It is a creative act in-volving the effective use of one's self as instrument. Preparing teachers is not a question of teaching them "how." It is a matter of helping each to discover his own best ways. The problem is not,

What is the right method? but, What is the most *appropriate* method to fit the individual's personal perceptions of the following?

1. The nature and content of his subject;
2. What he believes his students are like;
3. How he sees himself;
4. His own and society's purposes;
5. His understanding of the nature of the learning process.

If there were but a single factor to be taken into consideration under each of the five headings above, the task of finding the "right" methods appropriate to these categories would be within the realm of possibility. But within each of these categories there may be hundreds of variations, and the chances of finding the right methods become astronomical. Even the behaviors we call "habits," which most of us are used to thinking of as repetitions of an action, are now described by psychologists as never being done the same twice. Each human behavior is a creative act, a reaction of a person to the situation he sees himself to be in. So it is with methods. Each teacher must find his own best ways of teaching. To make this discovery most effectively, student teachers need

1. Rich opportunities for involvement with students and with teaching;
2. Concurrent opportunities to plan for such experiences and to discover the meanings of them after they have occurred;
3. An atmosphere that actively encourages and facilitates self-involvement and personal discovery.[1]

A FACILITATING, ENCOURAGING ATMOSPHERE

THE IMPORTANCE OF FEELING SAFE

For most people there is a natural reluctance to giving self over to untried and unknown circumstances. When one is involved, one

---

[1] Irvine reporting on the Project I studies of Buffalo, Syracuse, Cornell, and Rochester universities states, "Project I is concentrating on the differences in prospective teachers with a view to helping each student discover ways to use his unique self in the competent performance of a variety of roles as teacher-scholar." W. L. Irvine, "Project I: An Experimental Program for the Preparation of Secondary School Teachers," in *Changes in Teacher Education* (Washington, D. C.: National Commission on Teacher Education and Professional Standards, N. E. A., 1963).

is also vulnerable. When one is committed, one can be hurt. Many young people have been sufficiently humiliated in their previous experiences both in and out of school to make them approach with caution new situations which hold a potential for further self-damage. They have a real need to play things safe but the discovery of methods requires of the student that he risk himself. As we have already seen in our discussion of the atmosphere for learning, such exploration is most likely to take place when the individual feels safe and secure. Only the foolhardy take risks which are not likely to pay off. It is important, then, that a warm, friendly, understanding, and encouraging atmosphere characterize all aspects of the student's exploration of methods. Every effort must be expended to make his experiences as challenging and unthreatening as possible. Students should be given major responsibility for their own learning, and encouraged to "stick their necks out" in all kinds of experimentation and to dare to get involved to the very limits of their capacities. If this is to happen, however, it will require a high-grade staff of sympathetic people, able to provide support and assistance when needed and skilled in protecting students from humiliation, embarrassment, and failure.

Since it is the student's self which must be fashioned into an effective instrument, the atmosphere for personal exploration must begin with an acceptance of the self the student brings with him. It is the function of professional education to produce changes in the self, to be sure. There is a world of difference, however, in a program which begins by giving the student a feeling that his self as it stands is enough for now and can be helped to become adequate, or a program which diminishes and degrades the self by continual harping upon its insufficiencies. Acceptance of self, as any psychotherapist is aware, is essential to personality change. One can only progress from where he is. He cannot start from where he is not. So it is necessary that professional students begin with the feeling, "It is all right to be me," and "This self with which I begin can become a good teacher."

The atmosphere we seek involves accepting each student's self as it is, including his preconceived notions about teaching. Instead of rejecting these out of hand, they are taken as the place where this student begins and are accepted, considered, discussed, tried, tested, and modified by his own experience. Each person's own beliefs about teaching serve as his point of departure.

The principle of readiness which governs so much of what teachers do in their daily jobs must also be applied to the teacher's own experience in learning to teach. Teachers-in-training need to explore and try out what they are ready to do. The methods with which they experiment need to be those they can feel comfortable with and with which they have a chance of success. No matter how clever or sophisticated a method may be, its value to the student is dependent upon whether it works *for him*. The things which will *not* work for a given personality are so many that it does not really pay to explore them. The precious time available to help a student become a teacher is much better spent on things that fit than things that do not.

It is important, also, that the consideration of methods be approached in relaxed fashion. It is not necessary that all possible ways be considered or tried or even thought much about. Too much pressure to make a choice, especially if it must be the "right" one, may have the effect of impeding any choice whatever. Who has not had the experience of walking into a bookstore or record store and being so swamped with the thousands of choices available that he walked out again without buying anything, or worse still, with a purchase he didn't really want? The opportunity to try a few is much more likely to be helpful than standing immobilized before a thousand, unable to make a choice. Record and bookshop clerks have learned from experience that the browsing customer is more likely to buy than the hurried one. The same principle seems true when applied to shopping for methods.

THE IMPORTANCE OF ELIMINATING BARRIERS

To bring about an atmosphere conducive to the personal exploration and discovery of techniques, instructors need to root out barriers which lie in the path of such exploration. It goes without saying that a program oriented about helping the individual find himself has no room for invidious comparisions or competition among students. Learning to be a teacher is a developmental task of increasing uniqueness. As with an artist, we cannot compare his pictures with others'. We look at the changes occurring from picture to picture of one artist and value each artist for his difference from others.

The failure of students to understand the personal character of methods may create an additional barrier. Most beginning students share the commonly held conception that there are "right" methods of teaching. This belief may seriously interfere with the very learning we hope to produce. When methods are stressed, the student's attention is directed to the wrong place for solving his problems. When methods are practiced, it is methods which are the center of attention, rather than the goals of teaching. Psychologists point out that only one thing can be in the center of attention at one time. With attention centered on method or procedure, the teacher cannot properly respond to the individual needs of students with whom he is working or to changing conditions in the classroom which call for changing techniques. It is even possible that preoccupation with methods may seriously interfere with the student's success as a teacher. The use of kinescopes by which student teachers could see themselves in action, for example, did not produce noticeable differences in skill.[2]

There is a little rhyme I remember from my youth:

> The centipede was happy quite
> Until a toad in fun
> Said, "Pray, which leg goes after which?"
> That worked her mind to such a pitch
> She lay distracted in a ditch,
> Considering how to run![3]

So it is with teaching: over-concern with method may get in the way of the smooth operation characteristic of good teaching.

Actually good teachers are rarely concerned about methods. It is a fascinating thing to watch an expert teacher, doctor, or counselor as he goes about his work. He thinks about problems, ideas, goals, purposes, beliefs, understandings, and proceeds about his business by doing what comes naturally! His methods are like language. They are the expression of his thoughts, hopes, and goals, not chosen from his bag of tricks and applied. He operates by a kind of ad-libbing, adapting to events as they occur. The methods he employs flow naturally out of his knowledge and understanding of the problems and the goals he has in mind, so that what he does has a quality of "of course." It is appropriate. It fits. This genuineness opens lines of communication with students, creates a stable "expectancy" in

[2] H. Schuler, M. J. Gold, and H. E. Mitzel. *The Use of Television in Teacher Training and for Improving Measures of Student Performance. Phase I, Improvement of Student Teaching.* Mimeographed (New York: Hunter College, 1962).

[3] Mrs. Edward Craster in *Pinafore Poems* (1871).

the minds of students, and makes the teacher "visible" and human. Preoccupation with methods seriously interferes with these important aspects of the teaching relationship. An understanding of these principles about methods can save beginning students many headaches and lead to more efficient use of time and energies.

Common misconceptions about children may often create additional barriers to exploring techniques. One of these is the belief that children are basically evil, the natural enemies of adults. With such a feeling about his pupils, the beginning teacher can hardly afford to do much experimenting with methods. Seeing children on the other side of every question, he is likely to be so busy hanging onto his power and authority that he does not risk trying anything new. It often comes as a great surprise to student teachers that children can be trusted, that most of them are not scheming to embarrass or destroy their teachers. Even some experienced teachers never get over this fear, even after fifty years of service. The fact is, however, that children, like everyone else, want to be adequate. They even *want* to learn if they can be freed to do so. They really want the same things their teachers do for them—to grow up to be worthwhile, important people.

Another misconception has to do with children's fragility. They are often assumed to be delicate and likely to be irreparably harmed by any single thing a teacher may do. This notion has been fostered by some psychologists' stress upon the traumatic events in a child's life. The consequence of such emphasis on trauma has been to make many parents and teachers afraid of children. It is interesting to see how many teachers who fear doing something that will destroy a child at the same time will hold an equally firm, but inconsistent, belief that the child is entirely the product of his parents and what teachers do does not matter! Actually, what teachers do does matter, but not so much that any one event is likely to destroy a youngster. Children are tough, and can take a great deal. If they could not, they would never grow to adulthood.

Finally, it is essential that the atmosphere for exploring methods be one which values and encourages experimentation. It must give students the feeling that mistakes are of minor consequence and the really important thing is trying. Whatever gets in the way of the freest possible opportunities to experiment, even with the wildest, most far-out notions, should be eliminated. Students who are afraid to experiment fall back on the methods used on them. This is not so bad when those methods fit, but the attempt to adopt someone else's methods when they do not fit can be disastrous.

When students are afraid to try, they rely on crutches of one sort or another, like the age-old advice to beginning teachers, "Start out tough! Don't let them get away with a thing!" Unhappily, once having come to rely on such crutches, some students are never able to give them up. The future of the profession is dependent upon the production of teachers deeply ingrained with the experimental attitude. It should begin with the very first teaching experiences.

PERSONAL INVOLVEMENT WITH STUDENTS AND TEACHING

For a very long time our teacher-training programs have operated on a philosophy of "preparing to teach." Students were taught the "good" methods or "right" methods with the expectation that after they had learned them well, they would then apply them, first in practice teaching and then on the job. For most students this meant little or no contact with live students until the day they entered the classroom for their practice teaching experience. Practice teaching was regarded as a kind of examination at the *end* of learning rather than a learning experience in itself. This is a dreadful waste of a wonderful opportunity.

Participation in teaching should be the occasion of learning, not of testing methods after learning is finished. Young teachers ought to be involved with students and teaching at every step of their training in all the ways we have already suggested in Chapter 3. The laboratory for the student teacher is interaction with people in all kinds of settings and particularly in educational ones. Long ago we learned that the gradual approach to teaching children to swim or breaking horses to the saddle was superior to throwing them in the water, or riding the bronco down. In similar fashion the learning of methods needs to be a slow process of discovering solutions to problems and one's own best ways of working. This calls for continuous opportunities to be involved in teaching activities rather than a single traumatic plunge at the end of professional training. Ideally, this kind of program would begin with students "helping" teachers at the very outset of their professional training, with the time and responsibilities involved smoothly increasing throughout the period of professional training.

Each teacher-education curriculum can give different kinds of opportunities for involvement, depending upon local conditions. Some programs make full use of these opportunities, but others are not even aware of what resources exist in the local area, beyond those officially established for practice teaching or internship experiences. A great deal more imagination needs to be devoted to searching out and contriving involvement experiences for all students in every phase of their training and at every level of participation, whether it be observation, working with single individuals, with small groups or with large classes.

In recent years we have come to appreciate the importance of early involvement for quite another reason. Increasing technology and industrial automation has created a world which demands more and more knowledge and skill of all our citizens in order that they will be able to pull their proper weight. We have also launched a national effort to eliminate poverty, and we are looking to our public schools for ways of helping persons from every class of our social system to achieve the maximum of which they are capable. These are bold and exciting goals. Whether we achieve them will depend very largely on our success in training teachers to work effectively with the most needy of our citizens.

This calls for teachers who are ready and able to get out of their familiar ruts and confront aspects of the world they did not know existed. In the past we have characteristically drawn our teachers from the upper middle class. Many of them do not know what it is to be poor, or hungry, or rejected, or subjected to minority group pressures like discrimination. Yet many of these teachers will find their first positions working with just such people. We cannot afford to prepare them to teach in a world that does not exist. To help them discover their own best ways of teaching, they need to be immersed in educational and human problems just as deeply as they can take it, with the security and help of friendly persons around them to help when the going gets rough and to provide encouragement and assistance as it is needed.

THE PERSONAL APPROACH TO SUPERVISION

The "self as instrument" concept of good teaching calls for a new conception of the role of supervisors in the education of student teachers. The task of supervisors is usually conceived as one of helping students learn how to teach. Often such instructors are chosen because they are master teachers able to teach extremely well. This very expertness can, however, get in the way of helping teacher-education students to discover their own best ways of teaching. The supervisor's task must be to help another person find *his* best ways of teaching. Lindsey comments on this point:

> Being a master teacher does not, by itself, qualify one for leadership in the field of teacher education. To work with the prospective teacher as a colleague in guiding learners calls for special competence, no small element of which is the ability to teach "through" another person. Many a master teacher finds it very difficult, if not impossible, to share his skills with a novice, to recognize and appreciate ways of guiding learning other than his own, to safeguard the interests of learners, while at the same time giving the teacher-to-be, freedom to "try his wings."[4]

The master teacher who conceives of his job as a matter of helping the student learn to teach as he does will defeat the very purposes of teacher education as we have outlined them in this book.

Conant suggests the use of "clinical professors" as supervisors of teachers-in-training. These are persons "prepared by training to understand what other specialists have to say, and inclined to listen to them, and prepared by continuing experience in the elementary or secondary school to demonstrate in concrete teaching situations the implications of expert judgment.[5] There seems much merit in this suggestion. Supervisors who do not themselves engage in front-line activities can all too easily slip into the trap of teaching students *about* teaching rather than helping them find their own appropriate ways of teaching. Indeed, this error is so easy to make that even active involvement in teaching will not of itself insure escape from it.

It is a rather frustrating experience to ask a good teacher about his methods because he often cannot tell you about them. Since he rarely thinks about methods, questioning him about them is very likely to be embarrassing because he probably believes he *should* know good reasons for his behavior. Consequently, he will make up some for you which will almost certainly be *only parts* of the real reasons. Let us

---

[4] Margaret Lindsey, *New Horizons for the Teaching Profession* (Washington, D. C.: National Commission on Teacher Education and Professional Standards, N. E. A., 1961).

[5] J. B. Conant, *The Education of American Teachers* (New York: McGraw-Hill, 1963).

take an example of a good teacher whom we have observed doing "just the right thing" with a child. She behaved the way she did because, among other things, of the ways she saw him, how she saw herself, how she saw the problem the child faced, how it looked from his point of view (empathy), how she saw the rest of the class, how she was feeling, how she felt the child was feeling, where they were in the lesson, where they were in the hour, how far along this child had come in his studies, what he is ready for and what is too much for him, and so on. Impressed with what she did, we ask her, "Miss Brown, why did you do that?" The answer we get is not at all why she did that. She tells us why she thinks she *must* have done that! What we get is a psychologist's explanation of the historic reasons bearing on the problem, the child's performance, past history, what he needs, *some* of which had a bearing on what she did, to be sure, but which are only a pale excuse for the warmth, color, vitality, and sparkle of the real thing. A preoccupation with what teachers do may only serve to point the student's attention to the wrong places for change and destroy the effectiveness of the supervisor as well.

FOCUSING ON CAUSES RATHER THAN RESULTS

Formerly, we have conceived the task of the supervisor as a "critic teacher," someone who would assist the student to evaluate his performance and find new and better things to do. Emphasis was on the teaching act, what the teacher did. The effect of this concern with the student's behavior, however, is to focus attention on results rather than causes. As modern psychology tells us, behavior is only a symptom of internal states of feeling, seeing, believing, and understanding. To help people change behavior, it is on these factors we must concentrate. This calls for a shift in the basic orientation of supervisors. Instead of focusing attention on what students *do,* they must learn to concentrate on how student teachers feel, think, believe—about themselves, their students, their purposes, and the subject matter they are charged with teaching.

Supervisors in many other fields have learned they are more likely to get results by bypassing the question of methods to deal with the more important questions of the student's beliefs, feelings, and understandings. The counselor-trainer, for example, explores with the student such questions as "How do you feel about your client?" "How do you suppose he feels about that?" "What is it you are trying to do in the time you have with your client?" The supervisor sees his role not as one of teaching methods and techniques, but of helping the student-in-training to explore his own perceptions and beliefs about the critical questions which govern his behavior. Supervisors in teacher education must learn to be concerned with similar problems.

To help students in this way calls for supervisors who are more than master teachers. They must also be skillful in establishing warm, nonthreatening relationships with student teachers and must possess clear understanding of what is needed to be truly helpful in assisting students to explore and discover their own best ways of operation. This calls for supervisors whose own thinking about what is important and what constitutes good teaching is clear and enlightened. They will also need to be people capable of much self-discipline so that they do not make the mistake of imposing their own values on those whom they are supervising. In addition to being knowledgeable in their own right, persons chosen for these kinds of responsibilities will need to be people with respect for the dignity and integrity of others, who will value difference, and who are able to respect the right of student teachers to find their own best ways.

RICH OPPORTUNITIES TO EXPLORE AND DISCOVER APPROPRIATE TEACHING TECHNIQUES

The "self as instrument" concept of professional work which I have advocated in this book requires helping the student find and use the very best methods of teaching which will suit him. Teaching methods is a question of helping students explore and discover purposes, technique, self, and subject matter. These must be encountered as a whole, not in unrelated bits and pieces, as the discovery of methods is not a matter of putting things together in the most logical form. Rather, it is a question of finding those techniques which best fit a unique individual operating in a complex and changing set of circumstances. To my mind, this calls for a laboratory approach to the question—a workshop type of operation.

What is needed is not courses in methods, but curriculum laboratories, places where curriculum materials are available in abundance and where students can explore and try out all kinds of equipment, supplies, and materials. Such laboratories may operate in close conjunction with libraries, but should also provide space for experimenting with materials needed by teachers in carrying out their jobs. They should also be available when students need them, open at all times so that students can browse as they wish or work by themselves or with others. There should even be opportunity, if the student wishes, to set up materials and leave them for a period of time while he continues to experiment with them. Some medical colleges now provide small offices within the college assigned to medical students. Working in their own offices, students can get the feel of professional work in a professional setting. Perhaps the day may come when we will regard similar facilities as important aspects in the training of teachers as well.

Teachers-in-training need to be surrounded with rich opportunities to see the kinds of methods and materials other people have found useful. This can be provided by observing teachers in action, by opportunities to examine curriculum materials through reading, demonstrations, and the whole gamut of audio-visual devices now available to us. It is important, however, that the student be given opportunities to explore these materials at his own speed and in terms of his own needs and without prejudice. The moment labels of "good" or "bad," "right" or "wrong," become attached to methods and materials, students are no longer free to explore at will. The pressure to be on the "right" side restricts choices. Worse still, if he has the misfortune to be seduced into trying a method which does not fit him, he may reject the method forever because "it doesn't work" when the real difficulty was that he wasn't ready. The student subjected to many such experiences may even end with the conclusion that his instructors "don't know what they are talking about," that "educational theory won't work," or that "this progressive education jazz is 'for the birds.' "

An attitude of critical appraisal should reign in the laboratory in order to avoid either blanket acceptance or rejection of methods. There *are* things that can be taught very well by lectures, television, teaching machines, and the like. There are also things that cannot. To deal with all methods as dichotomies—as though they were good or bad—only compounds the problem and makes it less likely that we will find adequate solutions. Good teachers cannot afford either to go overboard for a method on the one hand or to resist what it honestly can do on the other.

The kind of laboratories we have pleaded for in the paragraphs above, where students can be free to experiment in whatever ways they choose, will provide important opportunities for students to interact with each other, to see what others are doing, to involve themselves in argument and discussion, and to test ideas in the open market place. Additional opportunities for this kind of exploration can be provided in the various kinds of demonstration and group discussion activities provided by the college as a part of its regular curriculum. We have already discussed some of these group activities in previous chapters.

The supervisor or teacher of the kind of laboratory we have been describing will himself have to be a first-class teacher with a wide variety of skills, sensitivity to the needs of students, and an enthusiastic willingness to share himself and his skills with student teachers. The kinds of teaching he does should be demonstrations in action of the best he knows about teaching so that students not only talk about teaching techniques but experience them as well. What is more, the supervisor should be sufficiently secure so that he can permit, and even encourage, students to critically examine his methods and procedures without fear of reprisal. At our university it is interesting to note that when students come in from their field experiences or internship, they do not ask to see the expert teachers in our Laboratory School. They want to talk to each other about very practical matters of the most elementary sort. It takes real understanding on the part of supervisors to let students be and to set aside their own pet methods and ideas while helping a beginner find his. All things need to be open to discussion in the curriculum laboratory, including the supervisor himself.

In the search for personal techniques for teaching, there should be no unreal distinctions between what is good for public schools and colleges. Teacher-preparation programs are often criticized because some of the things taught, particularly in classes preparing elementary teachers, seem a far cry from traditional college procedures. Education students learning children's games, learning how to make papier-mâché figures or number boards for teaching arithmetic, or gathering files of useful materials are sometimes disdainfully regarded by nonprofessional students as engaging in "Mickey Mouse" activities. But every profession has its simple techniques as well as its profound and scholarly aspects, and one is no good without the other. Such criticism should not dissuade the teacher-preparation programs from engaging in whatever is necessary for the production of teachers. Whatever is useful and helpful, no matter how simple or bizarre, should find its proper place in the curriculum laboratory, as long as it contributes to the exploration and discovery of useful techniques for the students involved.

9

Organizing the
Professional Aspects of a
Teacher-Preparation Program

So far in this book we have been exploring the bases for an effective teacher-education program from current knowledge about learning and behavior change. But how would one go about constructing one? What would it look like? At the present time there is no existing curriculum which incorporates all the elements about which we have been speaking. Here and there, there are programs which seem to point in promising directions, but none has all the answers. What is more, it is unlikely that any one program ever will. Teacher-education programs, like teachers themselves, need to serve local needs and purposes. There will probably be very few opportunities to build new programs from scratch. We shall have to be content with encouraging institutions to examine assumptions, to eliminate local barriers to change, and to push forward wherever possible to new ways of producing better teachers.

The definition of what a teacher-education program ought to be is not a matter for one man to decide. Since this is a free country, however, there exist no serious restrictions on ideas. One can still speculate as he pleases, and one man's speculations may provide a ferment to the thinking of others. With this hope in mind, I am emboldened in the rest of this chapter to set down, for what they may be worth, some suggestions for how the professional phases of a teacher-preparation program consistent with the principles I have outlined might be placed in operation.

THE INADEQUACY OF ORGANIZATION AROUND CONTENT

A curriculum primarily concerned with content lends itself to a neat hierarchical organization in which materials can be presented step by step in sequential order. Various prerequisite arrangements can be established to control the entrance of students to courses. This is the traditional pattern of course offerings existing in the typical liberal arts college department of mathematics, biology, chemistry, and the like. It is also the organization taken over years ago by most teacher-preparation programs for their own use. Unfortunately, it is most inadequate for our modern purposes.

A sequential structure of courses makes some sense when content is the essential matter to be dealt with. Professional education, however, is not a discipline in its own right. It represents the application of a number of other disciplines. Its content is drawn from many sources. There was a time when a teacher-education program could be neatly cut up into separate pieces like a pie (see Figure A). The professional college could be similarly divided into departments or courses, each responsible for its own bit of the overall function. Various members of the staff could also be assigned to clear-cut tasks. Some could be responsible for teaching human growth and development; some for teaching the relationship of school and society; some, philosophy of education; some, methods of teaching English, social studies, reading; and some, practice teaching. With an emphasis upon content and methods this kind of organization made sense and resulted in fairly efficient administrative operations. Job descriptions could be clearly determined and staff members selected who could carry out these neatly described tasks.

Changes in our conception of the learning process now demand a shift in emphasis from content to the learner, and the traditional organization of the teacher-preparation program is no longer adequate. The pie-shaped organization of former years has been disrupted by the emergence of the learner at the center of the learning problem. All educators are concerned with the middle of the pie. The "nature and condition of the learner" has invaded every course (see Figure B). With everyone concerned about the learner, subject matter that formerly was the exclusive prerogative of the course in human growth and development has now invaded the entire curriculum. *Everyone* now teaches human growth and development. Similarly, with the

FIGURE A   *The Former Teacher-Preparation Curriculum*

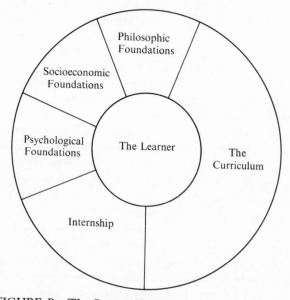

FIGURE B   *The Present Teacher-Preparation Curriculum*

learner at the center of the problem, everyone must teach the relationship of the individual to society, the purposes of education, and the utilization of effective methods. It is no wonder that many students complain of repetition in professional education courses! We have not yet learned to organize our program in accord with our new goals.

The inadequacies of the old content organization become even more glaring in the light of the concepts of learning and of good teaching on which this book is based. Learning conceived as the acquisition of content means that the individual can be continuously presented with new material as rapidly as he can assimilate it. Learning as behavior change calls for the discovery of personal meaning. Professional preparation requires a deeper grasp of basic principles as well as the acquisition of new data. It may therefore be necessary to consider the same content repeatedly to help the individual examine and re-examine its meanings in a deeper and more personal sense. This often proves a very distressing experience to inexperienced professional students, who find themselves examining the same data in several classes. Most of their previous experience in school has taught them that "you are not learning anything unless you are acquiring new information." They do not yet understand that it is the student's use of himself as an increasingly effective instrument, rather than the content, which is crucial in a professional program.

THE NEED FOR FLEXIBILITY

A professional program built upon the "self as instrument" concept must break out of old traditions which sought to provide *common* experiences. Maximum flexibility is called for. To provide this kind of flexibility we will first have to shake ourselves loose from the lock-step of some of our traditional ways of organization. The familiar concepts of courses, credit hours, classroom scheduling, grading practices, examinations, and the like may often be helpful in organizing learning around content. They may also seriously interfere with producing a change in *people and their behavior*.

An efficient program must

1. Permit the movement of students at different speeds;
2. Provide content and experience in response to student needs;
3. Provide simultaneous, rather than sequential, experience for the learner;
4. Place much more responsibility upon the student himself.

The professional program must provide opportunities for students to move at varying rates of speed. Anything less is wasteful and inefficient. We advocate increased flexibility in public education so that children may move at their optimum rates. Can we, in good faith, do less for our teachers-in-training? The good teacher is not a finished product, but a human process. This process may be observed at various stages of development, but it is never complete or finished. People come to us at various levels and move at varying rates of speed. The teacher-education curriculum does not *produce* teachers. It would be more correct to say that it "begins" them. It enters the life of the individual for a short period, helps him orient himself, and turns him loose on his own once again. This means the adequate program must be prepared to pick the student up at whatever point he has reached on entrance and carry him forward as far as possible in the time he is with us. This is not easy, but it is possible.

The adequate professional program will also be geared to student needs. There is little point in teaching what the student cannot grasp or what he already knows. These are principles which everyone in education knows and agrees with. Yet throughout the teaching profession there is probably no principle more often violated. It is so much more convenient to handle students as though they were alike, even when we know they are different. If, however, we are to make any headway in helping teachers apply what is known about individual differences in their classrooms, we must show them good examples in their own training. Where else but in their own experience can this be more appropriately demonstrated?

The concept of the good teacher we have been talking about calls for a simultaneous, rather than a consecutive, order of experience. The perceptual aspects of the good teacher that we described earlier do not take place one after the other, but simultaneously. As one changes his views about the nature of people, he also changes his conceptions of his relationship to them. Such changes in turn have their implications for the ways in which the individual perceives his purposes and procedures. Methods, too, will change with changes in the individual's ways of perceiving himself, his world, and his task. The self of the teacher is an interdependent organization, not a series of isolated boxes which can be dealt with one at a time.

If the person of the teacher is seen as the center of the problem of teacher education, the organization of teacher-education programs around subject matter and methods is simply no longer tenable. The definition of the good teacher we have been talking about does not lend itself to this kind of neat packaging. A problem-oriented, personal-growth-oriented program flows over all boundaries.

For the program we envisage, it will be necessary to place much more responsibility for learning on the student himself. We shall have to trust students more. We shall have to grant them a larger responsibility for their own education than some colleges have been willing heretofore to contemplate. Responsibility is the very essence of the professional worker. Responsibility, however, is learned from being given responsibility. It is never learned by having it withheld. A program of professional training must treat its students as responsible people and encourage the growth of responsibility through independent action on the part of students. To achieve such a goal the teacher-training curriculum will need to give very careful attention to at least three major principles:

1. It will need to expect and demand that its students take an active part in their own education. Students must be treated as responsible, independent, mature persons. From the beginning of their professional training they must be treated as professional people, able to make decisions and accountable for their consequences.

2. It will need to involve students intimately in the planning and direction of their educational experiences and programs. This seems essential for the kind of responsibility we seek. Students must be given a voice in matters that concern them and opportunities to consider and plan for further experiences. A program built around student needs which does not involve students in the business of planning seems an anomaly indeed.

3. The college will need to provide the administrative, instructional, and physical facilities for encouraging individual and small-group communication and experimentation in every way possible. The faculty and its administrative staff will need to examine their facilities with an eye to eliminating the barriers to interaction and personal involvement, on the one hand, and actively seek to encourage involvement, on the other. It must be recognized, too, that barriers to student interaction and communication are by no means all physical. Administrative rules and regulations, originally conceived to facilitate the

achievement of certain purposes, have a way of developing an autonomy of their own and continuing to exist long after the purposes they were meant to facilitate have changed to something else.

A PROPOSAL FOR ORGANIZATION

To develop a professional program meeting the criteria we have been considering in this book, we need a great deal of experimentation. Colleges everywhere must be encouraged to seek new and fresh approaches to our problems. Some have already begun this search and their experiments are indeed promising. Among them are San Francisco State College,[1] the Universities of Rochester and Buffalo, Syracuse University, Cornell University, and Hunter College.[2] At the University of Florida, many of my colleagues have been involved in experiments with our undergraduate program,[3] and a new program beginning at Florida Atlantic University promises to be most interesting.[4] While none of these studies fits all of the concepts discussed in this volume, all are most provocative. Combining their experience with the thinking involved in this work, I have asked myself, What might happen if we were to organize a program based upon the three principles of 1) providing information, 2) providing for involvement, and 3) providing for personal exploration and discovery? What would happen if we were to design a program to meet as many as possible of the criteria which I have indicated in this book? In the pages to follow, I have suggested a plan that strikes me as a possibility for the undergraduate or pre-service program. I recognize that some aspects may be too radical a departure to suit some readers. In that case, I suggest that the interested reader develop his own.

[1] F. T. Wilhelms and A. E. Siemons, "A Curriculum for Personal and Professional Development," in *Changes in Teacher Education* (Washington, D. C.: National Commission on Teacher Education and Professional Standards, N. E. A., 1963).

[2] W. L. Irvine, "Project I: An Experimental Program for the Preparation of Secondary School Teachers," in *Changes in Teacher Education* (Washington, D. C.: National Commission on Teacher Education and Professional Standards, N. E. A., 1963).

[3] I. J. Gordon, J. E. Blackburn, R. L. Curran, D. S. Laird, and W. Olson, "The Florida Experiment in Undergraduate Teacher Education," in *Changes in Teacher Education* (Washington, D. C.: National Commission on Teacher Education and Professional Standards, N. E. A., 1963).

[4] *Program Announcement, 1964–65* (Boca Raton, Fla.: Florida Atlantic Univ., 1964).

Suppose we were to organize the professional aspects of teacher education in such fashion that each student would be engaging in three kinds of experiences all the time: exposure to ideas, involvement in practice, and the discovery of personal meaning.

THE DISCOVERY OF PERSONAL MEANING—THE SEMINAR

At the very center of the professional program would be provision for the continuous exploration and discovery of personal meaning. This might be provided through a series of small group seminars under the leadership of an instructor or team of instructors who would serve as advisers of seminar students while they remained in college. Each seminar would contain fifteen to thirty students, depending upon staff availability and the best student-faculty ratio the program could afford. Each student would be assigned to a seminar when he entered the program and would keep this assignment throughout his professional program. Formal meetings of the seminar would be two hours a week for the entire period of the student's professional training. These hours could, of course, be quite flexible depending on local needs, but I chose a two-hour period because this lends itself best in my experience to serious group discussion operations. From time to time, as students left the seminar for whatever reason, they would be replaced by new entering students, keeping the seminar at a constant size. Thus, the group might be composed at a given time of students at all levels of progress. So long as he remained in the teacher-preparation program, however, the seminar would be the student's home base.

The purpose of the seminar would be to provide a group small enough for students to have adequate opportunities for discussion, and stable enough so that there would be ample opportunity for them to get to know each other and to be known by their seminar professor-advisers. Every attempt would be made to create an atmosphere of interest and concern for students and continuous involvement in professional matters. Here the student would be given opportunities to discuss, experiment, explore ideas, techniques, concepts, and the like with the friendly assistance of the permanent staff leader and such other consultants as the leader might bring in from the remainder of the faculty as needed.

In the seminar, students would plan their own work and chart their own directions with the guidance and supervision of the seminar leader. They would be involved in continuous evaluation of their current status and where to go next, culminating eventually in the decision to undertake the internship. For some this might be quite early, for others, perhaps, not till the very end. One would hope that because of the stability and intimate relationship between students and staff leaders that a good deal of counseling would be carried on both in and out of the seminar. We know that young people are extremely hesitant to discuss their problems with strangers, and the provision of a friendly ear and a stable relationship with someone on the staff might make it possible for more effective counseling of most students than we have heretofore been able to provide.

The particular program of the seminar sessions would grow out of the needs of the students in the group. It would also be affected by the other experiences of the students in the "exposure to ideas" and "involvement" phases of the program. Ideas confronted and needs created in those experiences would provide much of the basis for discussions and explorations in the seminar groups. With skillful leadership these seminar groups might be involved in all sorts of activities, sometimes breaking into smaller groups, sometimes working alone, sometimes together depending upon needs and the nature of the problems to be explored. In recent years we have made great strides in understanding group discussion and workshop ways of working.[5] Many of these have real promise for educational use. Seminar leaders would be chosen for their skill in such ways of teaching.

Ideally, these seminars and their supervisors ought to be provided with permanent laboratory facilities in which they could meet, hold discussions, experiment, set up and tear down exhibits, gather and catalogue materials, and so on. It would be a delightful thing if each student could be provided permanent space and facilities in such a laboratory. This is probably asking for the moon, but some lucky institutions might be able, at least, to provide each student with locker space within such a laboratory, so that he might use the laboratory as a place to study, experiment, and work with small or large groups from time to time when the seminar was not formally in session.

No doubt, the idea of having students remain in such a program for variable lengths of time will seem to many educators a highly questionable innovation. If, however, we are going to develop a

[5] E. C. Kelley, *The Workshop Way of Learning* (New York: Harper, 1951).

program to meet the needs of students, it will be necessary for us to recognize that since needs are variable programs must be. From my own experience in the training of counselors I have found it works quite effectively to have the supervisor and the counselor-in-training decide when the student is ready to take on an actual case. When I first started this system years ago, I was fearful that students would enter into competition with each other as to who could start this experience sooner. I was surprised to discover, however, that these comparisons were not made. On the other hand, much was gained in the increased security of students, who only took on the responsibilities of counseling a person when they were really ready to do so. I believe such an organization for teachers-in-training would prove similarly successful.

Another innovation which will probably raise some eyebrows is the organization of these seminars in such a fashion that beginners would be entering a group already in existence. There would thus be wide differences in the levels of operation of students in the group. However, it seems to me essential that we move in the direction of assisting students to take much more responsibility for their own learning if we are to meet the tremendous influx of students in modern education. If students really take on such responsibility, wide differences in the levels of competence are of no concern. For the older students in such a group, what more valuable experience could they have than opportunities to teach the new ones coming in? On the other hand, newcomers entering the group will have the effect of forcing older members to re-examine their procedures and assumptions periodically. This seems all to the good.

THE EXPOSURE TO IDEAS

The second type of experience provided for students in training would be designed to make maximally available the resources of the community and the faculty for exposing students to ideas. This would involve a wide variety of experiences aimed at providing information, stimulating thinking, airing controversies, confronting students with professional problems, demonstrating methods and techniques, or giving students opportunities to see and hear persons with important things to say for educational thought and practice. Some of these sessions might be required of all students. Some would be established in response to the needs of particular groups. Others would simply be made available to students without requirement of any kind. Some experiences provided in this phase of the students' preparation might be planned long in advance, others might be set up on comparatively short notice. To assure that all students and staff members were informed as to resources available, a calendar of events would be provided and revised as often as necessary to be maximally useful. Using this calendar, the student and his adviser would determine between them which events the student would be *required* to attend, which he might *choose* to attend, and which he could safely *ignore*.

Some of the kinds of experiences provided in this portion of the training program would be the following:

A College-Wide Lecture Series. These sessions, open to all personnel in the college, would be planned by a student-faculty committee appointed or elected for the purpose. Such a planning committee would be composed of faculty members representing different phases of the college program and students elected from the seminar groups. Some of the sessions in this lecture series would be planned and announced long in advance. The most important value in a student-faculty planning committee, however, lies in the machinery it provides for relating program to student needs by presenting information at the time it is needed. Many programs, therefore, would be established on comparatively short notice in response to the particular needs of students at a particular time. In this way, lectures, demonstrations, or whatever was required might be quickly arranged under the leadership of whichever members of the faculty could most effectively deal with the problems.

I first began thinking about the use of planning committees to determine content some years ago when I began a search for ways to make my lectures more related to the needs of students in large classes. Accordingly, I set up a planning committee composed of students elected from our discussion groups. These delegates met with me every two weeks and reported on the kinds of things their respective groups wanted to hear about. After hearing these reports, the committee and I would then determine the topics to be covered in the next lecture or two. In this fashion, I was able to construct lectures much closer to the immediate needs of students from week to week. Over the years I have found an additional advantage—this technique has the effect of keeping the instructor much more alive! Some of the requests of these committees are highly similar from year to year but I find they appear in quite different order. Many other requests are quite unique, leading me to develop ideas and presentations in directions I would never have been stimulated to explore by myself. It even happens, on occasion, that the planning committee suggests that they would rather hear from someone else—a most sobering experience! I am indebted to these committees for removing much of the dullness that could otherwise creep into a tried and true set of lectures dished up year after year. I feel certain a similar technique could be applied to the lecture series we have been discussing here.

Some of the events that might be included in such a lecture series, would be the following:

1. Lectures by persons on the faculty who have particularly pertinent things to say or who are effective and talented speakers. In many teacher-training programs the insistence upon all instruction occurring in small classes sometimes results in a program in which students may go through their whole college career and never have the opportunity of seeing and hearing outstanding members of the faculty because they were never assigned to a course he taught.

2. Imported speakers brought to the lecture series from outside the college faculty. Some of these sessions might be planned long in advance, others would be planned on short notice in order to take advantage of the presence of important people who happen to be in the community for other reasons.

3. Panel discussions arranged to deal with important and interesting topics. These would not be restricted to faculty. They should certainly include appearances by students as well. In my own teaching I have sometimes used panels of elementary and high school pupils discussing all manner of problems from their own point of view. This can prove to be a fascinating experience for teachers-in-training as they have an opportunity to see how things look from the other side of the fence.

4. The whole range of modern audio-visual techniques offers tremendous possibilities for information programs. Movies, television, tape recordings, slides, all these can be effectively utilized in large group situations.

5. Finally, such college-wide lecture series sessions should be available to the students themselves for their own purposes, whatever these may be.

Limited Group Presentations. It is neither appropriate nor efficient for all exposure to ideas to be presented through college-wide lectures. There will, of course, be need for smaller group programs from time to time, attuned to more limited objectives: for example, orientation programs for beginning students, commencement sessions for graduating students, special sessions for students about to go out on internships, and so on.   Other limited groups may be organized around ideas, people, or subject matter of interest to smaller groups of students, such as the implications of a given point of view, theoretical position, or controversy or a series of lectures by a particular professor on a topic of peculiar interest to him.   These limited group sessions would also be planned by the student-faculty committee proposed in our discussion above.

Special Workshops. From time to time special workshops would be set up growing out of common needs experienced by one or more seminars.   These would make available to students with common problems such special resources from the college faculty as could be of assistance in those matters.   They would run for comparatively short periods and be concerned with the solutions to fairly limited problems.   They would be established in response to requests from the seminar sessions.

Exhibits. From time to time important exhibits would be arranged within the college to acquaint students with educational resources of many sorts.   These might include art exhibits, book exhibits, exhibits of special interest in history, government, community resources, methods and materials for teaching, and a thousand other possibilities.

Trips. Certainly an important resource in a teacher-training program are trips so that students may see at first-hand some of the things they hear and read about.   Any college has a wealth of opportunities for learning within a reasonable radius of its campus.   Many of these have important educational value and should be widely utilized.

THE PROVISION OF PRACTICAL EXPERIENCE

The third phase of our proposal would be organized to involve students actively with young people, both in and out of schools, and with professional affairs in a wide variety of settings.   Some of this involvement would be planned to occur simultaneously with the seminar sessions. Some might be planned to alternate with such sessions, depending upon the availability of resources and the demands of efficient use of time and energy.

Practice Teaching. The kind and duration of practice teaching experiences for any student would depend upon his needs and the particular skills he had already acquired. Ideally, a student would begin as a teacher-helper, spending perhaps a half day a week at the very beginning of the program and gradually increasing his role and responsibility until by the time of internship he would be in full charge of a classroom for at least a four-month period. The purpose of this involvement is three-fold: 1) as an important learning experience in itself, 2) as an experience for the creation of needs to know, and 3) as an opportunity for the student to try himself out in a practical laboratory. In traditional programs, practice teaching for students has often been seen as an opportunity for the student to try out his teaching *after* he has learned how. In the program we envisage, the practicum is also valued for its contributions to motivation of learning throughout the teacher-education program.

The kind and amount of practice teaching required of each student in our plan would be determined by the student and his seminar adviser on the basis of all the information available about the student's current needs and status. Thus, some students might spend much longer than others in an observational level of participation before entering an actual classroom situation. It is even conceivable that some phases of the participation program might be eliminated entirely as, for example, in the case of the sensitive, middle-aged mother entering the profession.

In the paragraphs above we have spoken of student involvement primarily as teacher-helpers or an internship experience. However, there are at least four other kinds of involvement that ought to play a part in an efficient teacher-education program. These are the following:

A Program of Observation. While observation is a kind of arm's-length involvement, it can often serve a very important purpose in helping to raise questions in the minds of observers. It can also provide important opportunities to see how other people handle events, and it may develop in the observers sensitivity to problems of the classroom. Observational opportunities for teachers-in-training have long been provided by many by education programs, usually with the idea that students should observe only master teachers in action. Accordingly, many teacher-training programs have demonstration schools for the purpose of providing for such observations. As we have seen earlier in this book, a knowledge of the methods of the experts is not necessarily very helpful to the neophyte. Indeed, it may be only discouraging. While observing a teacher "way out" from one's own position may be stimulating or shocking, a steady diet of this sort of thing is unlikely to be very helpful. Since the task of the teacher-in-training is to produce some change in himself, it would appear that there might be important values in having the student observe especially those teachers with whom he can identify.

Of all the places in teacher education where television has important possibilities, none seems more significant than the use of closed circuit TV for observations. The teaching possibilities inherent in sitting down with a class in one room to watch and discuss the activities of a teacher and his class in another room are tremendous. No one disturbs anyone else, and discussion and observation possibilities are limitless. With such facilities available a whole seminar group could make the same observations at once and discuss them on the spot. One excellent description of such a seminar approach to observation is that suggested by Sarason[6] and his colleagues.

Involvement in Young People's Groups. Teachers-in-training can learn a great deal about young people from involvement in all kinds of activities outside, as well as within, the school. Involvement in youth groups often has the additional advantage of providing the young teacher with opportunities for community service. Many professional programs encourage education students to act as helpers in youth groups such as Girl Scouts, Boy Scouts, boys' clubs, city recreation programs, private nursery schools, YMCA and YWCA groups, Little League baseball, and craft shops.

Involvement in Professional Affairs. Another place in which young teachers may steep themselves in professional life is through attend-

[6] S. B. Sarason, K. Davidson, and B. Blott, *The Preparation of Teachers* (New York: Wiley, 1962).

ance at teachers' conventions, local meetings, and the like. Here, they may have an opportunity to rub elbows with people in the profession and learn much by a process of osmosis that could not be taught in a classroom setting. Other school-related activities can also provide important opportunities for involvement. Among these are attendance at school board meetings, school board election rallies, school budget meetings, PTA meetings, and all kinds of school functions put on by the students themselves.

Involvement in Educational Research. On many faculties there are important opportunities for student involvement in research projects of their own. There is nothing quite like involvement in research for the development of proper critical attitudes toward research findings or for helping students acquire a real research orientation to educational problems.

ADMINISTRATIVE PROBLEMS OF ORGANIZATION

The first reaction on looking at a program that departs so widely from many of our existing procedures may be to throw up one's hands in despair at the administrative problems involved. However, whether or not such a program is administratively convenient ought not determine whether we make the effort. The acceptance or rejection of an unorthodox program should be based on a more valid reason than expediency. The only valid criterion, in the final analysis, must be, Does it produce better teachers?

One of the most serious problems to be solved in organizing such a program is the matter of faculty responsibilities. In most education programs the teaching staff is typically assigned responsibility for a given "class load." This class load is usually made up of four or five three-hour courses, taught to anywhere from ten to two hundred students. Why all courses should always be three hours in length has never been quite clear to anyone, but so they remain as a matter of tradition. The course is the traditional unit around which the program is organized.

We have seen that this pattern of organization no longer makes sense. Many of the perennial problems plaguing programs of education arise from our outmoded organizational patterns. Most programs, for example, have serious problems of "overlap" and staffing, most of which come from a rigid adherence to the old content orientation. Professional education is seriously hampered by the necessity of pouring it into the rigid forms of the traditional liberal arts organization, which does not fit the peculiar needs of a professional program. A program for the preparation of teachers must be much more dynamically oriented around the *person* of the student. It is time we recognized this need and found the courage to break with tradition sufficiently to put the principle into effect.

How the faculty is utilized in the professional education program should be a function of the peculiar talents of the staff member and the needs of the program. It is people and talents that make a program, not courses and hours of exposure. It is wasteful and inefficient to use faculty members in places they don't fit or to fail to use the peculiar talents they possess to the fullest possible extent. I have known colleges where nationally renowned lecturers were never heard by students of their home colleges simply because all courses were limited in enrollment to thirty and nobody in the college ever lectured to groups larger than that. On the other hand, I have also known teachers bored to tears by their teaching assignments while some of their colleagues died of envy wishing they might have a try at them. Then there is the instructor with ten good lectures in him who must teach a class which calls for thirty. Can we not find a way to release both teacher and students from the boredom of those extra twenty? Let us discard this Procrustean bed and find ways to fit the needs of *both* students and faculty.

If we do this, some staff members will need to be kept for graduate programs and special lectures or consulting roles. Some will have to be utilized in administrative and supervisory roles. Some, whose peculiar talents make them effective workers with small groups, should certainly be working in this fashion. Some we will need for seminar leaders, counselors, research supervisors, or placement officers. Some staff members may even be used in varying combinations of the above. While the staffing problems of a teacher-education program are difficult, they are by no means insurmountable. It is necessary, however, to think in terms of time and skills and most effective use. We need the same kind of flexibility in thinking about staffing problems that we have called for in providing for student needs. The important problem is to fit the peculiar talents and contributions of each faculty member into a smoothly operating team.

STUDENT EVALUATION

The traditional liberal arts pattern for evaluation has been concerned with the student's mastery of a particular body of content. The professional aspects of teacher training, however, are only in small measure a question of the mastery of content. Rather, they are concerned with student growth toward becoming a teacher and this, as we have seen, is a quite different matter indeed. Mastery of content is only a part of what goes into the making of a good teacher. The traditional use of grades, therefore, as indications of success in the acquisition of subject matter makes no sense applied to professional education. What, then, is the place of evaluation in the preparation of teachers?

Evaluation in professional education is needed for two purposes: 1) Some kind of final evaluation is called for at the conclusion of training to indicate the degree of promise the student shows as a prospective teacher. This is primarily a service to prospective employers when the student is faced with acquiring his first job. Sometimes this evaluation has been done by the simple expedient of averaging all the student's grades. While the assignment of course grades may represent a convenient indication of the degree to which the student has mastered a given body of subject matter, the assignment of grades to the kind of evaluation a college places upon a student's promise seems highly questionable. It is indeed a shame if, with all the richness of the American language, we are reduced to evaluating a student's promise in terms of A, B, C, D, or F! The college placement office is keenly aware that this is by no means enough and so requires much fuller descriptions of students to supply to prospective employers. As a consequence, the placement office, whose contact with the student may be for no more than ten minutes, knows him better than the college which has lived with him for four or five years! One wonders why we don't just give up grades and adopt placement office evaluations.

2) The second kind of evaluation needed in the professional program calls for indications to the student of his current status so that he may see where he is and where he needs to go next. This is a diagnostic evaluation which has nothing to do with the question of passing and failing. It is a matter of the assessment of growth and the determination of direction. Students need many opportunities throughout their experience for exploring what it is they need to know, where they need to go, and how they may go about getting

there. In the plan we have proposed, this would take place in the seminar or with the student's adviser. It would not happen at a fixed point or be expressed in a formal grade. It would occur whenever it was needed and would be explored in a counseling relationship. Even more important, the evaluation would deal with the problem of "What can I do about it?" rather than "Where have I fallen down?" It would be an evaluation for treatment, not a judgment of worth, as grades so often become.

It is commonly assumed that grades have high motivational value. Actually, they do not, except perhaps for the day before they are posted and the day after. It is well known to teachers, that grades only motivate those students who think they can win. The rest sit back and watch the grade worshippers beat their brains out. Donald Snygg once defined grades as "artificial motives we give students to get them to do things they never would if we didn't!" Grading may actually impede professional education because it takes attention from the real problems and focuses it upon the importance of outguessing the instructor. Professional growth is not dependent upon self-analysis, but on how effectively the self is used. To this end, invidious comparison with others is no good, for the need is not to be like others, but to become increasingly and effectively oneself. While grades may have values for the teaching of content (by no means certain), they certainly have little place in the preparation of teachers.

The kind of evaluation most likely to be effective is that produced through counseling, in which the student may explore with his supervisors where he needs to go next in his training program and how to get there. This conception of evaluation will no doubt prove distressing to many a college registrar, who will find difficulty in fitting such information into his IBM machines. Registrars, however, are not supposed to determine the evaluative practices of a professional program. If necessary, to keep him happy, however, we can always supply his machines with a grade at the student's completion of the professional sequence by marking the student "pass" or "fail." Meantime, we can get about the business of producing effective teachers, which is our primary function, after all.

Index

Academic-professional dilemma, 25, 39
Acceptance and learning, 35
Acceptance of self, 100
Adequacy:
  need for, 16
  self-concept and, 15
Adequate personality, 16, 61, 69, 72, 77
  production of, 73
Administration of teacher-education program, 117, 127
ALLPORT, G., 23
Anthropology, 87, 90
ASCD, v, 35, 70, 79
Atmosphere for learning, 34, 96, 99, 100, 119
Audio-visual materials, 109
Audio-visual techniques, 123
Authority, earned and unearned, 69
Barriers to learning, 101, 117
Behavior and knowledge, 25, 28
Beliefs and good teaching, 54, 62
BENTON, J. A., 20, 54, 84
BILLS, R. E., 24
BODE, B., 47
BOWERS, N. D., 4
BRUNER, J. S., 45
BUFFALO, UNIVERSITY OF, 92, 118
Capacities, 61
Causation, 107
Challenge and threat, 35, 100
Clinical professor, 106
College organization, 113
COMBS, A. W., 2, 18, 20, 24, 35, 54, 70, 75, 79, 84, 85
Commitment, 28, 78

Communication, 48, 62, 64
  failure of, 26
Competencies, practical difficulties, 4
"Competencies" approach, 2, 13
CONANT, J. B., v, 106
Concepts about people, 54
Conformity, 35
Content:
  organization of, 47, 90, 113, 117
  and practice, 25
  psychological, 60
  selection of, 39, 40
  structure of, 45
  and student purposes, 47
  in teacher education, 39, 44, 88
Content specialization, 43
CORNELL UNIVERSITY, 92, 118
Counseling, 70
Counseling program, 79, 120
Course organization, 113
Creativity, 35
Critic teacher, 107
Culturally deprived, 105
Curriculum for teacher education, 113
Decision groups, 93, 95
Democracy:
  concepts of, 86
  education for, 93
Demonstration school, 126
DENEMARK, G. W., v, 42, 75, 80
Detail, 45
Discipline of self, 71
Discovery of methods, 108
Discussion groups, 37, 92, 110
DIXON, W. R., 18

Educational psychology (see Psychology, educational)
Elementary teacher, 44
ELLENA, W. J., 3
Empathy, 58, 64
Environmental treatment, limitations of, 58
Evaluation, 120, 129
and grades, 130
Experience:
order of, 116
organization for, 124
Experimental approaches, 100
Experimental attitude, 37, 103
External frame of reference, 55
Facts in teacher education, 45
Faculty responsibility, 117, 127
Faculty-student planning, 122
Family relationships, 61
FATTU, N., 4
Fear of children, 103
FIEDLER, F., 17
FILSON, T. N., 4
FLANDERS, N. A., 4
Flexibility, need for, 115
FLORIDA, UNIVERSITY OF, 19, 92
FLORIDA ATLANTIC UNIVERSITY, 118
Frame of reference, 55
Freeing-controlling, 85
FREUD, S., 11
FROMM, ERIC, 24
General education, 43
Generalization, 62
Goals, 32
GOODING, C. T., 20, 54, 60, 71, 85
GORDON, I. J., 92, 118
Grades:
and evaluation, 130
and grading, 46
and learning, 50
Group discussion, 66, 92, 119
Habit, 99
Helping relationship, 17, 61
Historical view of causation, 55
HODENFIELD, G. K., 25, 44

HUGHES, M., 3
Humanistic psychology (see Psychology, humanistic)
Ideas, exposure to, 121
Identification, 70, 78
Immediate-historical causation, 55
Individualizing instruction, 116
Information and teaching, 48
Information explosion, 40
Instrument, self as, 8, 10, 98, 105, 115
Internal frame of reference, 55
Internship, 30, 33, 104, 110, 125
Involvement, 29, 33, 37, 85, 88, 99, 104, 117, 119
and sensitivity, 64
in subject matter, 49
IRVINE, W. L., 92, 99, 118
ITTELSON, W. H., 24
JOHNSON, V. B., 45
JOURARD, S. M., 24
Judgment and professional work, 75
KELLEY, E. C., 24, 66, 69, 120
Knowing:
and behaving, 25, 28, 87
and understanding, 51
Knowledge and teaching, 20, 26
KOERNER, J. D., 39
KUENZLI, A. E., 24
Laboratory, teacher-education, 108, 120
Laboratory schools, 126
LANE, H., 24
Language, seduction of, 87
Learning:
atmosphere for, 34
barriers to, 101
conditions for, 31
and grades, 50
nature of, 27, 51
organization for, 115
as perception, 59
and purpose, 22
Learning groups, 94
LECKY, P., 24
Lecture series, 122
Lecturing, 72

LINDSEY, M., 19, 29, 43, 75, 106
LYNCH, W. W., 19, 78
McCLENDON, P. E., 19, 78
MASLOW, A. H., 24, 72
Master teacher, 106
MAY, R., 24
Meaning:
  and content, 45
  discovery of, 37, 94
Meanings-facts orientation, 55
MEDLEY, D. M., 4
Methods:
  of good teachers, 102
  personal discovery of, 108
  of teaching, 23, 65, 98
  uniqueness of, 7
Misconceptions about children, 103
Models for teaching, 4, 33
Motivation, 16, 32, 55
MOUSTAKAS, C. E., 24
NCTEPS, vi, 29
Need:
  basic, 16
  and learning, 32, 61
Needs:
  of society, 41
  of students, 116
  of teachers, 42
Objectivity:
  in observation, 64
  in selection, 74
Observation program, 125
Observations in teacher education, 64
Openness to experience, 70, 78
Organization:
  of content, 90
  of programs, 112, 127
  of teacher education, proposals for, 118
Peer relationships, 61
People-things orientation, 55
Perceiving and behaving, 61
Perception:
  effects of threat on, 34
  and good teaching, 18
  and learning, 59

  and need, 32
  about people, 20
  of self, 22
Perceptual basis of behavior, 12
Perceptual psychology (*see* Psychology, perceptual)
Personal approach:
  to methods, 98
  to supervision, 105, 107
Personal meaning:
  and learning, 37
  and teaching, 27
Personality, the adequate (*see* Adequate personality)
Philosophy, 63, 90
  of education, 86
  and psychology, 57
  and purpose, 84
Placement, 129
Planning committee, 122
Practice teaching (*see* Internship)
Problem solving, 53
Problems approach, 88
Problems oriented program, 117
Professional-academic dilemma, 25, 39
Professional judgment, 75
Professional program, 112
Psychology:
  educational, 11, 56, 62
  existential, 12
  humanistic, 11
  organization of content, 60, 90
  perceptual, 12, 58
  psychoanalytic, 11
  stimulus-response, 10, 11, 56
  Third Force, 11
  traditional views, 56
Psychotherapy and teaching, 17
Purposes, teacher's, 22, 82
RAMSEY, C. P., 19
Readiness, 105
Research, 127
Responsibility, student, 100
Responsibility for learning, 117
ROCHESTER UNIVERSITY, 92, 118
ROGERS, C. R., 17, 24

Role description, 91
Ryans, D. G., 19
San Francisco State College, 92, 118
Sarason, S. B., 30, 66, 126
Scholar-practitioner dilemma, 24, 39
Schuler, H., 102
Scientific method, 51
Selection of students, 73
Self:
    and methods, 100
    positive view of, 70
    of the teacher, 68
Self as instrument concept, 8, 10, 98, 105, 115
Self-acceptance, 100
Self-actualization (see Adequate personality)
Self-analysis, 76
Self-concept, 15, 61, 77
    and behavior, 14
    and teaching, 22
Self-discipline, 71
Self-disclosure, 68, 84
Self-discovery, 34, 36
Self-perceptions, changing, 76
Seminar, teacher-education, 119
Sensitivity and involvement, 64, 110
Simmons, B., 92
Smith, O., 4
Snygg, D., 70
Social foundations, 86
Social needs, 41
Social purpose, 23, 84
Sociology, 87, 90
Soper, D. W., 2, 18, 54, 70, 84
Staff responsibilities, 128
Structure of content, 45

Student evaluation, 129
Student responsibility, 117
Subject matter (see Content)
Sullivan, H. S., 24
Supervision, 105, 120
Syracuse University, 92, 118
Teacher:
    defined, 9
    as knower, 1, 42
    as a person, 6
    self of, 68
Teacher education, "competencies" approach to, 2
Teacher-education laboratories, 104, 108
Teacher-education program, 112
    administration of, 117, 127
    organization of, 113
Teacher-education seminar, 119
Teaching:
    and need satisfaction, 33
    perceptual view of, 10, 18
    personal approach, 6
Teaching act, 107
Teaching machines, 109
Teaching methods, 23, 98
Teaching relationship, 17, 20, 103
Teaching task, 16
Teaching techniques, 98
Team teaching, 91
Television, 67, 126
Testing for selection, 74
Third Force psychology (see Psychology, Third Force)
Threat and challenge, 34, 100
Traits, 4
Values and teaching, 63
Wilhelms, F. T., 92, 118
Workshops, 124